PREACHING GOD'S WORD ON SUNDAY

*To the memory of
Marie McAteer
1916-1996*

Desmond Knowles

Preaching God's Word on Sunday

HOMILIES AND PRAYER OF THE FAITHFUL
FOR YEAR A OF THE THREE-YEAR CYCLE

the columba press

First published in 2004 by
the columba press
55A Spruce Avenue, Stillorgan Industrial Park,
Blackrock, Co Dublin

Cover by Bill Bolger
Origination by The Columba Press
Printed in Ireland by ColourBooks Ltd, Dublin

ISBN 1 85607 459 5

Table of Contents

Acknowledgments

A book like this would not be possible without the help and support of several people. Many thanks to those good friends who have given generously of their time in proof-reading these homilies as well as those who offered honest and valuable criticism. I am deeply indebted to Celine McAteer who composed the Prayer of the Faithful for each weekly celebration and which flows directly from the theme of the particular Sunday homily.

Introduction

St Francis of Assisi instructed his followers to 'Preach always, sometimes with words', indicating the power of good example, which is within everyone's reach. However, priests and deacons are mandated to preach 'with words' and in this book I have been mindful of the obligation to share 'the unsearchable riches of Christ' (Ephesians 3:8). Preaching is both a privileged and a humbling activity requiring prayerful and careful preparation. One of the greatest challenges to the preacher throughout his years of ministry is to take what he knows from his study of theology and express it in a language that can be understood by his congregation. Its content must be something that awakens a living faith in worshippers so that they may turn their minds and hearts towards God and be renewed in their commitment to Christ's call to discipleship. Jesus used language that evoked images and appealed to the imagination. So should we. By connecting the 'Good News' of the gospel with the real-life concerns of the congregation, the preacher is giving his listeners encouragement in their daily lives. The homilies contained in this book are the result of my preaching experience over a period of seven years as an emigrant chaplain in Paris and five years as a parish priest in Ireland. A single theme has been chosen for each homily since the preacher generally has around seven minutes at his disposal. My hope is that this collection of homilies may provide a stimulus for thought and be of some help in the understanding of the faith and in the search for God.

First Sunday in Advent

First Reading: Isaiah 2: 1-5; Second Reading: Romans 13:11-14;
Gospel: Matthew 24:37-44

Advent is upon us again and another year of Christian worship begins with the story of the coming of the Lord. It affords us an opportunity to reflect on the longing and hope within the hearts of Jewish people for the arrival of a Messiah and Saviour. The birth of Jesus, which on the surface seemed an ordinary and everyday occurrence, was an event so far beyond expectation and belief that the Israelites needed a long period of preparation for it. During that time, God sent many messengers and prophets to instruct, guide, encourage and chastise his chosen people. And last of all, when the time was ready, the Almighty sent his Son into the world. Nothing like it ever happened before and nothing like it will ever happen again until Christ returns in glory.

We tend to see Advent as a past event, recalling the birth of Christ but if we fail to move forward from this starting point to Christ coming in glory, our Christmas celebration will be out of focus. A proper celebration of Advent recalls the past, celebrates the present, and yet looks to the future coming of Christ with joyful hope and confidence. Perched on the edge of another New Year we are invited to look at our world with the eyes of faith and realise that God has a plan and a vision for all of us.

The readings present us with a challenge, to look at life and to begin living with a new perspective. In keeping with the season's note of expectation, they rivet our attention on the breaking of God into human history. Isaiah's vision of a new future echoes in all our hearts as he looks forward with hope and expectation to glorious times ahead. He dreams of swords being cast into ploughshares, of unity among nations and of all peoples walking together in the peace of the Lord, who is calling us back home. It is an invitation addressed to each and every one of us. Paul encourages us to lead good and upright lives as the dawn of salvation is upon us. In the gospel passage, Matthew is referring to the final coming of Jesus in glory and sets his call on perpetual watchfulness, to be ready for that moment on which our eternal destiny will depend. Since there is no precise forewarning as to when that event will take place, it is important to get ready here and now and not be caught idly napping in careless disregard for God, as were the people in Noah's day who were swept away in the great flood. Things happen when we least expect. The main thrust of the message is to be vigilant, to rectify our way of life, to admit the need to make a Christian contribution and have a proper lifestyle. A useful reminder of something we would rather forget, is that part of the gospel tradition which tells us that each one of us after death comes face to face in judgement with our God. On that occasion we will be alone and held personally accountable for our life. Busy as we are with our daily activity, we tend to put the thought of that encounter at the back of our minds, giving it scant attention instead of using it as a benchmark and a horizon against which to measure our lives. The gospel warns us against being lulled into a false sense of security, living with only the minimal concern for how our actions appear in God's eyes.

Advent is a joyful celebration of the condition we find ourselves in as Christians. It announces that God is always moving towards us. He is at work in the world and in our lives, ever creative and ever renewing. The Lord comes to us every day if we are properly disposed, in prayer, in events and in other people. The good news is that we are pilgrims on the move and are going home to God's house. The only worthwhile baggage to carry on that journey is good works and acts of loving service performed for Christ. The liturgy invites us to allow this future hope to shape our present lives. It's an invitation to see our life as a preparation for the great call home. We have the assurance that in Christ God has opened up for us a future hope in a life beyond our time. This seasonal call proposing a deep change in values, beckons us to look forward to Christ's return in glory. We need to find the time and space to stop, reflect and recognise the hope we have been given in Jesus Christ. Without repentance, forgiveness and renewal there can be no real Christmas Joy.

Prayer of the Faithful

Celebrant: As we enter the Season of Advent, we place our petitions before God the Father as we await the coming of his Son, Jesus Christ.

1. That the Holy Father, bishops and priests may be aware of their unique mission of proclaiming Christ who is the light of the world.
    Lord, hear us.

2. As we prepare spiritually during these weeks of Advent, we pray that our hearts may be filled with joyful anticipation.
    Lord, hear us.

3. That the longing in our hearts for lasting happiness may be fulfilled by following our Saviour on the road which he travelled from the crib to the cross.
    Lord, hear us.

4. For the sick, the lonely, the discouraged and the heart broken, that they may find strength and hope in the love God has for each of his children.
    Lord, hear us.

5. That those who have gone before us, marked with the sign of faith, may now rest from their labours and that their good works may go before them.
    Lord, hear us.

Heavenly Father, you so loved the world that you sent your Son, Jesus Christ to redeem us. Help us to stand ready for his coming, so that we may rejoice forever in the happiness of heaven. We ask this through Christ, our Lord. Amen.

Second Sunday in Advent

First Reading: Isaiah 11:1-10; Second Reading: Romans 15: 4-9
Gospel: Matthew 3:1-12

The spotlight is on John the Baptist as a fiery desert preacher who captures the imagination of his fellow Israelites. He came on the scene when the people had been without a messenger from God for a long period. At an early age John was inspired by the spirit of God to leave home, go into the wilderness and adopt the lonely lifestyle of a hermit. There he settled down to an ascetical discipline of prayer, penance and fasting in the Palestinian desert around the region of the Dead Sea. As a recluse in the wilderness he gave his full attention to the word of God and the things of the spirit. The only interruption from this life of prayer was time out to preach to the crowds who travelled from the surrounding area eager to listen to his message. It was an extraordinary tribute to his charismatic power that people flocked long distances to hear him preach. His words carried little comfort as he spoke the truth bluntly, sparing no one and blasting everything that was false. Addressing the religious leaders who came out to be baptised he confronted them with their hypocrisy and chided them for their complacency in presuming that because they were children of Abraham, God would be on their side. John was foolhardy enough to describe the religious establishment of his time as a brood of vipers. He warned them that God's strict judgement was close at hand and that nobody's salvation was guaranteed. The aim of his preaching was to get back to basics by challenging people to look deep into themselves, to search for God and have concern for others. Apart from Jesus he was the most powerful religious force in the first century and is now one of the most revered saints in the church.

As a patron of the Advent season, John reminds us that if God is to come into our lives we have to prepare for his arrival by mending our ways. Through the words of Matthew's gospel we hear him calling us to conversion inviting us to take a journey inwards, to the spiritual self, which is thirsting and hungering for God. Unfortunately, the hustle and bustle of each day puts us under such stress that we are inclined to live on the surface of things with precious little time to reflect on what is most important in life. Christ's hope is coming to us all of the time and we receive it when we open the door to him in prayer but we should be careful not to let this living contact wither. We need to make this Advent journey to get in touch with ourselves and with our God.

Every age of Christianity has something to learn from John the Baptist and from his message about the need for purification of the heart and for making a new start. Conversion is a continuous and lifelong process so it is never too late to begin the journey or to pick it up where we left off. Advent promises us fresh possibilities, opens up new horizons and invites us into a world that offers a better way of living. As the weeks before Christmas pass, Johns' words echo in the emptiness of our hearts and we sense a need to reach out to God for grace and to give him a fuller place in our lives. It is a call to spend a little time contemplating the mystery of the Lord made man, which is the heart of the Christmas story.

This is a disturbing gospel, puncturing the pretence of those who have settled for a merely comfortable religion and are unaware of how far they have drifted from God. There is a struggle involved in making the life of Christ come alive in our hearts. Among other things Advent means admitting our sinful past, reaching out for divine mercy and seeing our work as an occasion for service. Every time we show compassion or work for peace and reconciliation we too are sharing in the Advent vision of John the Baptist. If we care to look, we can see this spirit of Advent reflected all around us in parents who sacrifice so much to meet the needs of their children, in home helps who care and share the pain of the house-bound and whose visits are a sacrament of God's presence. The spirit of the Lord is with us to give us the encouragement and the strength we need to make our surroundings more Christ-like. Advent is a time when the Lord's grace is poured upon his church so that we can all be renewed, refreshed and replenished.

Prayer of the Faithful

Celebrant: Having listened to the message of John the Baptist challenging us to renew our lives and bring them into harmony with the gospel, we now pray to our Heavenly Father.

1. For the Church, that it may always shine as a light in the darkness and be a path for all who seek the Lord in the midst of life.
   Lord, hear us.

2. For our community gathered here, that this Advent season will be a time of blessing, as we wait in joyful hope for the coming of the Saviour.
   Lord, hear us.

3. Let us prepare for Christ's coming by praying for a spirit of reconciliation between ourselves and those we have offended.
   Lord, hear us.

4. That the frail, the lonely and the sick may find in those around them the love, support and comfort they need.
   Lord, hear us.

5. That those who have recently departed this life may rest peacefully with God and may those who mourn their loss find solace and peace during this Advent season.
   Lord, hear us.

God of peace and joy, with humble hearts we ask you to hear our needs. Help us to know your will for each of us and accept in faith whatever it brings. We make our prayer through Christ, our Lord. Amen.

Third Sunday in Advent
First Reading: Isaiah 35:1-6a; Second Reading: James 5:7-10;
Gospel: Matthew 11:2-11

There seems to have been the slightest hint of confusion among John the Baptist and his followers as to who Jesus really was. John, whose only home since childhood had been the open desert, was languishing in captivity in Herod's dungeon cell and that was not an altogether nice place to be. John the Baptist, who had never known doubt, was puzzled and was having second thoughts about the identity of the Messiah because Jesus seemed different from what he had expected. Walled up in prison and waiting for a brutal and senseless death, he was wondering about Jesus because the truth and worth of his life's work depended on the answer. The tone of Jesus' message, indeed his lifestyle, differed so much from his own that it raised some doubts and misgivings. Was Jesus really the Messiah or had he made a mistake in pointing him out? A stern and committed man, John had his own idea of how the Messiah would appear and expected his arrival with fire and whirlwind to crush the foes of God, shake off the rule of Rome and rid Israel of the Scribes and Pharisees. To his distress John was getting reports that Jesus was making no move in this direction. Instead Jesus had embarked on a different style of mission and was turning out to be a substantially different Messiah than was expected. Unlike his recluse cousin, Jesus was mixing freely with his fellow Israelites and socialising with life's losers, the down and outs of Jewish society. He was spending his days journeying through the towns and villages of Galilee, preaching not the wrath of God but mercy, healing, reconciliation, forgiveness and love. Great prophet though he was, John was experiencing a crisis of faith and could not grasp the true nature of the Messiah's mission. Small wonder that he sent messengers to Jesus to enquire and find out who the Messiah was and why all these things were happening. Even though he was honoured with the task of announcing the coming of the Messiah, John was in the dark and couldn't grasp the true identity of Jesus.

We can almost sense the exasperation and the frustration of John's mind in the blunt question his followers put to Jesus. 'Are you the one who is to come or have we got to wait for someone else?' In his reply Jesus hearkens back to Isaiah who spoke of comfort, healing and love. 'Just tell John that the blind see, the lame walk, lepers are cleansed, the deaf hear' and let him decide for himself and draw his own conclusions. Jesus is saying: 'See what I have done, put your trust in me and don't lose heart.' The messengers return to John with joy and excitement at the good news that the Messianic age has dawned. The Messiah and Redeemer is in the world proclaiming that humankind can be saved and healed only by the power of God's love.

Like John we experience moments of darkness, doubt, despair and anxious expectation as events in our own lives, or perhaps in the life of one of our children, do not work out the way we had planned. When our hopes are dashed and our dreams shattered, we lose heart and the feeling that we are living in a wasteland with a bleak future may tempt us to look elsewhere for meaning. At these critical times we need reassurance to continue believing that our individual path in life is a walk with God, that our future is in his hands and is perfectly safe in his presence. No matter how hard and rocky the road, once we let God into our lives we experience his strength and are surprisingly filled with peace, freedom and joy. Every challenge undergone, every test passed, every cross carried makes us stronger. The message of Advent is that we should wait patiently for the Lord to come into our lives. Everything has its moment and being patient is part of the process of life. In a world filled with instant answers and quick fix solutions, it's hard to be patient. However, you can't rush nature and you can't hurry God. He works in our lives in his own time and takes nature's gifts and builds on them with grace. With our co-operation he can heal our wounds, free us from anxiety and give us a peace that the world cannot give. Just as Jesus invited John to trust in him, so does he call on us to be faithful in our life's work.

Prayer of the Faithful

Celebrant: As we wait in joyful hope for the coming of our Saviour, Jesus Christ, we confidently place our needs before God the Father.

1. That the leaders of the church will always keep faith and be a beacon of joy and hope in a troubled world.
   Lord, hear us.

2. We pray for those who live without hope and suffer loneliness, heartache or homelessness, that they might find comfort and shelter through the concern of others.
   Lord, hear us.

3. That the celebration of Christ's birth will bring a renewed desire into the hearts of all people to work for and live in peace with one another.
   Lord, hear us.

4. That parents may follow the example of John the Baptist in pointing out Christ and preparing his way in the lives of their children.
   Lord, hear us.

5. For all who have lived the word of God in their lives and have now gone to their eternal reward that they may rejoice eternally in heaven.
   Lord, hear us.

Father, in your love, listen to our prayers and make us, like John the Baptist, fearless and humble witnesses of your Son's teaching throughout the world. We ask this through Christ, our Lord. Amen.

Fourth Sunday in Advent
First Reading: Isaiah 7:10-14; Second Reading: Romans 1:1-7;
Gospel: Matthew 1:18-24

Advent is running out of time and Christmas is almost upon us. The readings invite us to step aside for a while from the hustle and bustle of the commercial word to reflect on the events leading up to that first night in Bethlehem some two thousand years ago. Matthew views the story of the birth of Jesus through the eyes of Joseph and gives us a remarkable insight into his personality. The ideal that Jesus expressed when he said 'Blessed are those who hear the word of God and keep it' was deeply challenged when Joseph learned the news that Mary, his betrothed, was pregnant. There was nothing straightforward about this situation since they had not been living together as husband and wife. It was traumatic news and Joseph wondered how this could be. Faced with such a real dilemma and a crisis of intimacy, he felt cheated, embarrassed, hurt, and left out. As he struggled with this extraordinary happening, his heart must have been heavy and his dreams shattered. However he did not act rashly but responded to the situation with a generous and open heart.

Afraid, confused and unsure he prepared his course of action and made a lonely decision. Being an honourable and upright man of God, he planned to act quietly and chose a way that would shield Mary from scorn and save her from public embarrassment. But before he put his plan into action Joseph was taken into confidence by the appearance of God's messenger who came in a dream to explain Mary's uprightness and the divine origin of the baby. Joseph listened to God's word and through the angel's message allowed his life to be influenced and directed to God's will and acted accordingly. As head of the household Joseph had the specific role of naming the child. Moved by God's inner prompting, he accepted Mary as his wife and adopted her child as his own.

There wasn't much that was comfortable and cosy about Joseph's decision to hear and obey the word of God. He was what we would describe as an ordinary working class man called on to respond to God's extraordinary plan. Like any parent he had to cope with the same fears, worries and bitter disappointments that come to every home. His relationship with God must have been close because in this time of crisis he trusted God's word and co-operated with God in a decisive manner. Anguished he may have been and he may not have understood all that was happening, but he had come to realise that the hand of God was in everything, taking care of all things and he put his trust in this power. He was open to the Spirit at work in his soul and ready to turn his life upside down each time he heard God's call.

We can learn from this aspect of his character how to respond to God who communicates with us in the challenging situations of life. Nowadays, the vast majority of people are unaware of the religious significance of Christmas. They view it as a break from work in the wilds of mid-winter. It is our destiny to live in a world of unbelief and confusion where difficulties arise at every turn. With God's help Joseph got it right and so will we. Once we believe like Joseph and humbly surrender to God, there is no limit to what he can achieve in our own very ordinary lives. Christmas is a time for remembering and showing gratitude to those people who helped us out during the year. Let's not forget to show them the recognition that they deserve.

The basis of our Christmas hope is that not only is there a God who made the heavens and the earth but he is here with us now in the flesh offering us peace and reconciliation. We all have something unresolved in our lives that quietly eats away at us, disturbing our peace and our ability to show true love for others. As we approach this great feast of Christmas can we say like Joseph that we are ready to rely on God's help and guidance when we sorely need to be reconciled to another family member? Joseph's silent presence in the gospel is a testimony of God's great love for all the poor, humble and just people down through the ages, who are quietly faithful to trusting and relying on God in good times and in bad. As Jesus said 'Blessed are those who hear the word of God and keep it.'

Prayer of the Faithful

Celebrant: Mindful that God the Father speaks to us in various circumstances, we pray that we may hear his voice and listen to his message.

1. That the church and all those who give direction within it will continue to be a light guiding the faithful on the way to everlasting life.
   Lord, hear us.

2. That those who are living under the shadow of fear and worry may feel the presence of Mary walking with them in their distress.
   Lord, hear us.

3. In this time of giving and receiving, may Mary's openness be an example to us of how to receive God's gifts and in our turn, share what we have with those who are in need.
   Lord, hear us.

4. That the sick and housebound may be helped by people with caring hands and loving hearts, helping to ease their burdens and comfort their distress.
   Lord, hear us.

5. We recall our friends who have gone ahead of us sealed with the sign of the cross and commend them to God's loving care in his eternal home.
   Lord, hear us.

Loving Father, you walk beside us on our earthly pilgrimage. Like Joseph and Mary, we long for the coming of your Son into our lives. Hear these prayers of your waiting people. We ask this through Christ, our Lord. Amen.

Christmas
First Reading: Isaiah 9:1-7; Second Reading: Titus 2:11-14;
Gospel: Luke 2:1-14

With the arrival of Christmas there is an unspeakable sense of exhilaration and happiness in the air. It's that wonderful time of the year when the bright star of Bethlehem sets the world aflame with its message of good news. The mysterious joy of the season is irresistible, and affects the whole tenor of life for weeks on end. Of course what makes Christmas special is the presence of children in the house. Words fail to express this natural and very human joy, which is unique in every family.

The festive season is celebrated in many ways with a rich variety of customs, traditions and legends associated with this special time. Falling as it does in bleak midwinter with the cold and frosty fog outside Christmas breathes life into the darkness and makes us concentrate on nearness and the warmth of love. Family and friends draw closer to each other at this time of year and gather to celebrate not just Christmas but also the ties that bind them together. One of the most joyful parts of the season is the return of family members making what is for some their yearly visit home. For those who are far away and unable to make the journey there is a heartfelt yearning and a longing to be united with their nearest and dearest. For most people the images of a quiet peaceful nativity are probably the strongest and warmest memories of our childhood faith.

Amidst the hullabaloo of the Yuletide festivities we must not lose sight of the first Christmas Day and the birth of Christ as a vulnerable infant in the simple trappings of a stable at Bethlehem. Otherwise we are emptying the feast of its original meaning and closing our eyes and ears to the message of Good News. The gospel describes the harshness of the situation into which Jesus arrived. How as a helpless baby, he was born outside the city gates, in a stable, a feeding trough for animals, the child of poor parents and his first visitors were shepherds. In this way he accepted us as we are, and identified with the outcast, the marginalised, the poor and lowly. Like the shepherds we ponder the mystery of the Christ Child, the Son of God entering our world as one of us, clothed in our human flesh with all its limitations and weaknesses. Just as the angels praised the glory of God made visible in the child Jesus with songs of joy, so too must we. In the mystery of the baby breathing in the manger we are reminded that God breathes his spirit into the darkness of our lives and opens up an everlasting future for us. The coming of Jesus among us can change our view of life, restore our sense of self-esteem, and enable us to be channels for bringing his love and peace to others. God entering our physical world makes everything in it holy and good and helps us realise that we are people of hope, waiting for something great to break into our lives.

Visiting the crib, we pause and say a prayer of thanks for what we have. Spending time there we can gaze in silent wonder upon the mystery of God coming into our world, embracing us with his love, stamping his image upon humanity and giving divine worth and greatness to every human soul. The delicate image of a new-born child who came in poverty teaches us that there is greatness in humility, glory in service and power in self-surrender. We can ask to become more like him and reflect his grace in the way we conduct our lives. If we live by what is best and noblest in the human spirit we value the things that Jesus treasured.

Yet even in this joyful season suffering and sadness do not go away. Christmas is an incredibly emotive time especially for those who have lost a friend or family member during the past year. There is the pain of absence in memories of times past and a life shared with a beloved. Then there are those who are poor or alone and those who are under pressure because of some misfortune or personal tragedy. We think of them in their suffering and make them part of our prayer. Christmas brings the assurance that, no matter how dark are the days, God wants to free us from worry and grant us a peace that the world cannot give. Whatever your circumstances, wherever you are and whoever you are with, I do hope that you are able to find happiness and joy in this Christmas season.

Prayer of the Faithful

Celebrant: As the light of Christmas morning dawns upon our earth and the glory of the Lord shines upon us, we pray to our heavenly Father and give thanks for the birth of his Son.

1. For the Holy Father and all people of goodwill that they may be blessed in their striving to establish peace in the world.
    Lord, hear us.

2. That our celebration of God's love for his people may bring harmony and peace into our lives.
    Lord, hear us.

3. We remember those who are far from home this Christmas and pray that they may find a welcome and support through the kindness of others.
    Lord, hear us.

4. We pray for our children. Keep them in your care and let no harm befall them or sorrow touch them.
    Lord, hear us.

5. Let us remember our friends and relatives who have died since last Christmas and who are in our thoughts this day. May the Prince of peace welcome them into his heavenly banquet.
    Lord, hear us.

Heavenly Father, whose light, love and happiness have been shown to us in this Christmas season, give us the grace to walk in your presence. We make our prayer through Christ, our Lord. Amen.

The Feast of the Holy Family
First Reading: Ecclesiasticus 3:2-6, 12-14;
Second Reading: Colossians 3:12-21; Gospel: Matthew 2: 13-15, 19-23

According to a legend, the chief of a Native American tribe, knowing that he was going to die, called his three sons to his bedside. 'My sons,' he began, 'I am not long for this world and soon one of you will be chief. I want each of you to climb our ancestors' holy mountain and bring back something beautiful. The one whose gift is most precious will become chief.' When the three returned from their search several days later, the first son brought back an extremely rare and beautiful flower, the second a nugget of precious gold while the third son brought back nothing. Making his excuse he said, 'Father, as I stood at the top of the holy mountain, I saw on the other side a land of fertile green pastures and crystal waters. I dreamt of our people settling there and establishing a better life. I was so immersed in my dream that when the moment came to return I hadn't enough time to bring something special back.' The old chief smiled and said, 'Well done my son, you will be the chief for you have brought our family the gift of vision for a better future.'

It is the Feast of the Holy Family and the readings are directed to enhancing family values, to having a vision and daring to dream of a shared future in God's family. Paul, writing to the Colossians, suggests that among the qualities that make family life pleasant and worthwhile are compassion, patience, gentleness and forgiveness. If we have the courage to be honest we might admit that there are certain aspects of our own family life that need to be improved. None of us chooses our family but who we are is largely determined by the kind of environment we grow up in. The circumstances of our lives are part of an unfolding mystery and the experience of belonging to a family is one that is shared by every individual. It is the natural and fundamental unit upon which all societies are built and within which the values and characteristics of the next generation are shaped and developed. Since family can include people living in such a wide variety of circumstances there is no set pattern to family life. As well as parents with children, there are also lone parents, childless couples, the separated, those who are widowed, grand-parents and single people who have no partners.

Modern psychology stresses the crucial role of parents in the early years of children's development and underlines the funda-mental challenge of showing constant love. It points out that the failure to express love to young people can have disastrous effects in later life. As children have a way of making constant demands and repeating activities, which gain them attention, good parenting is about the proper use of quality time by setting boundaries, showing love, praising efforts and not just success. St Paul has his own way of expressing this when he says, 'Over all these clothes, to keep them together and complete them, put on love.' Paul's advice is as applicable to family life today as it was 2,000 years ago, for whatever the fashion of the day might happen to be or whatever the age group, the essential clothing for every Christian is love.

There isn't a family that doesn't have its fair share of trouble from time to time. Suffering seeps under every doorway. When as families we are faced with unexpected sorrow and unbear-able stress, what better model can we call upon for inspiration and comfort than the Holy Family. Joseph's role was that of guardian and protector, while being a mother to Jesus was Mary's most important vocation. One of the most notable things about them as a family was that they had lots of problems. They lived all their lives in the deep shadow of the cross. During Christ's infancy they fled the country in fear and sought shelter in Egypt as refugees in order to keep out of harm's way and avoid the violence of King Herod. They were a family away from home, lost and lonely, terrorised and afraid. Things did not get any easier as Jesus grew up and until he breathed his last on the cross, scripture tells us that a sword of sorrow kept piercing his mother's heart. When we endure sleepless nights because of the violence in our own homes caused by alcohol and drug abuse, the Holy Family offers us hope in our pain and under-standing in our plight. To recognise their presence in our lives can transform our deepest fears. May God bless your family with health and happiness in the coming year.

Prayer of the Faithful

Celebrant: On this feast day, we make our prayer to God the Father hoping that the example shown us by the Holy Family may always reign in our homes.

1. For leaders of the church – may they always guide those under their care with the strength and constancy of Mary and Joseph.
   Lord, hear us.

2. That our homes may always be places where we feel free to share our troubles and anxieties as well as our hopes and joys.
   Lord, hear us.

3. That those who experience depression may be strengthened by the love and support of those who care for them.
   Lord, hear us.

4. For the sick and the suffering, especially those in nursing homes and hospitals, that their faith in God may strengthen them and give them consolation.
   Lord, hear us.

5. That all those who carried their crosses faithfully in this life, may reap the reward of their earthly labours in heaven.
   Lord, hear us.

Heavenly Father, strengthen the bonds of love in our homes so that, like the Holy Family, we may live in harmony and peace with one another. We ask this through Christ our Lord. Amen.

Second Sunday after Christmas

First Reading: Sir 24:1-4, 12-16;
Second Reading: Ephesians 1:3-6, 15-18; Gospel: John 1:1-18

When a child is born there is an indescribable sense of delight in the air among friends and family. Words are at a loss to express the joy and excitement that swells up in our hearts as we greet the newborn babe for the first time. The innocence and helplessness of the infant child creates feelings of warmth and goodwill among adults and children alike. Peak moments like this can lift people out of themselves and produce an extraordinary atmosphere of awe and wonder even among the most detached of individuals. That same sense of awe and wonder shines through this gospel prologue. The writer, St John, tries to come to terms with the fact that Jesus, who was with God from all eternity, should come into our midst as a man and share our life. As a gifted spiritual writer John puts pen to parchment and in poetic language celebrates the coming of Jesus in the everyday occurrences of our lives. It is a profound insight into the meaning and the work of Jesus. John remains in utter amazement that the infinite God, at a point in time, crossed an unimaginable border and entered our world as a human being. The Almighty, who called the universe into existence and through whom all things came to be, took human flesh and pitched his tent in our midst. John reminds us that there are two sides to the astonishing mystery of God becoming man. There is the descent of God but also the ascent of man: for in making little of himself, Jesus made us as precious as himself. God could have chosen to love us from a distance. However, being a God of love, gentleness and belonging which is the language of everyone who is poor, homeless, weak and powerless, he chose to join us on our human journey. He came to make his home in the human heart.

In this gospel passage John is at pains to point out that beneath the sketchy surface details of the birth of Christ there lies an overwhelming mystery. We ponder in amazement at the self-emptying of God, at the Almighty becoming the all-lowly, a child perched on his mother's knee, helplessly gazing out at us from a lowly manger. As we approach the crib, kneel down and embrace the mystery, the thought crosses our mind as to what the eternal God was thinking about when he decided to come among us. It was nothing less than a rescue operation to bring us out of the darkness of sin and bathe us in his own wonderful light. Jesus Christ became our brother for no other reason than sheer love and a desire to have us live in an intimate loving family relationship with him. Like a great star Jesus comes down from heaven, lights up our darkened world and enables us to glimpse the mystery through the cloud of uncertainty. We are a privileged people for God has moved in with us and we now bear his image and likeness.

While the coming of Christ opens up the possibility of everyone being in a harmonious relationship with the Lord, nevertheless our new life in Christ is a gift on offer that we are free to accept or reject. There has been many a heart and a home closed to him since that first Christmas night when there was no room at the inn. God will not force an entry into our hearts but has left us free to be born into his family, receive his life and inherit his kingdom. We have in our hands the power to withhold this gift of friendship. The door of the human heart has but one handle and the key is on the inside. We have been invited to share in the life of Christ and we should pray for the wisdom to make a generous response in faith so that we can say in all honesty that Jesus Christ is the light of our lives. If Christmas is to be a time of genuine spiritual celebration then we have got to take a look at our Christian roots and discover where we fit into the story.

Christmas tells us that it is in the ordinary happenings of life as lived around us that we find God. We have to look for him not just in the faces of family and friends but also where there is poverty, want and despair. We express the true spirit of Christmas best when we offer help to those in need and bring hope to those who are lost. In this way we become a beam of light and a ray of hope piercing the darkness that surrounds so many lives.

Prayer of the Faithful

Celebrant: Called out of the darkness of sin into the wonderful light of God, we confidently place our needs before the Father.

1. That the Holy Father and all church leaders may always have the courage to proclaim the gospel fearlessly and be the visible presence of Christ in the world.
   Lord, hear us.

2. We pray for everyone in our parish community. May they grow in your love and live in your peace.
   Lord, hear us.

3. That those who feel excluded or unwanted by society may find a welcome in our community of faith.
   Lord, hear us.

4. For those who mourn the loss of a loved one, may their grieving hearts be comforted.
   Lord, hear us.

5. We remember all who have died. Grant them eternal rest in your kingdom.
   Lord, hear us.

Heavenly Father, enlighten our hearts and open our minds to the values and qualities of life which your Son has brought us. We make our prayer through Christ our Lord Amen.

The Feast of the Epiphany

First Reading: Isaiah 60:1-6; Second Reading: Ephesians 3:2-3. 5-6
Gospel: Matthew 2:1-12

Traditionally the twelve days of Christmas come to an end with the celebration of the Feast of the Epiphany and the arrival of three kings at the stable in Bethlehem. The colourful and somewhat magical story of the Magi dressed in royal splendour, bearing precious gifts, mounted on camels, travelling across a desert, outwitting Herod and all the time following a star, has captured the Christian imagination across the ages. It's a lovely legend and a marvellous myth around which many stories and works of art have grown. Any national gallery of art worthy of the name will carry at least one painting of the adoration of the Magi among its religious collection. Christmas would not be Christmas without a visit to the crib and see the look of wonder on children's faces as parents point out Caspar, Melchior and Balthasar.

After all their journeying, the Magi are faced with unexpected majesty in squalid surroundings. We are left wondering at the shock they must have got when they were confronted by poverty where they expected grandeur. Instead of a royal court with servants, they found a rocky cave with shepherds, and in place of a throne they saw a manger where a baby lay on a bed of straw. This would have been a stumbling block for people of lesser faith. However, their hearts were open and their minds receptive because they saw and understood the profound meaning, which lay behind the simple scene in the stable. They found God shrouded in the mystery of human weakness and in an act of worship they offered the newborn child gifts of gold, frankincense and myrrh.

This exotic story of high intrigue is inexhaustible in its meaning and its riches can never be adequately fathomed. Matthew, the gospel writer, had this in mind when he told this marvellously embellished tale. He knew full well that it would set our minds wondering. Take, for instance, the fact that the Magi were outsiders and not from the Jewish tradition. Even today outsiders have the problem of not belonging in any community, of living on the periphery and being socially excluded because they are black, from the wrong class and not in possession of a passport.

While most of us would like to think ourselves as devoid of prejudice, facts do not always bear this out. At the crib there are no outsiders for Jesus extends a welcome to everybody. He rejects no one, makes no distinction between rich and poor and treats everyone as equals irrespective of class or creed. It's worth remembering that God can use outsiders and unbelievers to teach his people lessons about the breaking down of divisions and barriers. In his great scheme of things he calls us to be a church that is openhearted, outward looking and all embracing. There can be no more important message for today than that everyone belongs to God's family.

The journey of the Magi causes us to reflect on our own journey through this world. They were not wandering aimlessly, but were heading in a definite direction with a specific purpose in mind. In the course of their journeying there were many twists and turns that kept them alert, caused them to seek advice and frequently alter course but they persevered and kept moving steadily forward towards their intended goal. Just as the Magi spotted the star, we are called to read the sign of the times that will point to the right road and face us in the proper direction. All our lives we are pilgrims on a once made journey that one day will come to an end. In the deep heart's core we have an inner feeling that here on earth we are exiles who have no final resting place but we seek one that is to come. In the course of life we may travel across oceans, visit many lands and meet different peoples but the one journey that ultimately matters is the journey inward, into the place of stillness deep within one's self. To reach that place is to be at home; to fail to reach it is to be forever restless. The journey inward to that quiet place where one's life and spirit are united with the life and spirit of God is long and difficult but it is a journey worth making because it is about finding inner peace through intimacy with the Lord. When the Magi left for home they brought with them a treasure that far surpassed any gift they had brought. Knowing Jesus was the added richness they now possessed. Once we make Jesus king of our hearts, it will be our treasure also.

Prayer of the Faithful

Celebrant: Just as the Magi, at the end of their journey, knelt in humble adoration before the Lord, we now offer our prayers to God the Father.

1. We pray for the leaders of the church that the Lord will guide them in their efforts to bring Christ to all nations.
   Lord, hear us.

2. That the coldness of this wintry season will instil in our hearts a greater awareness of those who seek food and shelter.
   Lord, hear us.

3. For all who are searching for God, that by following the light of their own conscience, they may come to a fuller understanding of God's love for humankind
   Lord, hear us.

4. We pray for those who have begun this New Year in sadness. May they come to know the peace of Christ in their hearts.
   Lord, hear us.

5. May those members of our community who have died in Christ live forever with him in eternal life.
   Lord, hear us.

Heavenly Father, we thank you for revealing your Son, Jesus Christ, to us. Grant that we may be always open to his spirit of truth. We make our prayer through Christ, our Lord. Amen.

The Baptism of the Lord
First Reading: Isaiah 42:1-4. 6-7; Second Reading: Acts 10:34-38;
Gospel: Matthew 3:13-17

We may wonder why on earth Jesus insisted on being baptised. It is easy to appreciate the reluctance felt by John when Jesus joined the queue of sinners and presented himself for baptism at the river Jordan. It must have been an incredible scene as the sinless one of God, who was far greater than John and had no need of baptism, came forward. Stepping down into the muddy waters of the human condition was a statement by Christ that he was not standing aloof from sinners but had come to show solidarity with a suffering people and to identify completely with humankind. He embraced his vocation and was familiar with all the hardship we experience.

This was a turning point in the life of Jesus. It meant leaving behind his trade as a village carpenter and giving over his career completely to the work of God the Father, which was the reason why he was sent into the world. Baptism set Jesus up for his mission. Through the power of the Holy Spirit it signalled the start of his public ministry to preach the good news, heal the sick, raise the dead, cast out demons, give sight to the blind and light to those in darkness and in the shadow of death. The heavens opening in a blaze of glory indicated God the Father's seal of approval at the beginning of his Son's mission and ministry. The time had arrived to tell the world openly the good news of God's saving love and of our need for redemption. The reign of God, restoring his wounded and broken creation, had begun. The day Jesus was baptised not only marked the beginning of his ministry but our introduction into the Christian way of life.

After birth, the most important step in our lives is our baptism. It is a graced moment marking the beginning of our relationship with God. Sharing God's life means placing ourselves in his hands, walking in his company, belonging to his family, reaching out to others in need and being able to call God 'Father' from that day forward. Baptism is called the gateway of the sacraments, the entrance to the church and the door to the future. At our baptism our true dignity is revealed to us because we are freed from sin and reborn as children of God belonging to the Father, Son and Holy Spirit.

Baptism is not over and done with when the church ceremony is completed. It is the beginning of our faith journey for we have been chosen for a mission in the world of today. We are privileged to have a part to play in God's overall plan of salvation. Being a Christian involves making personal decisions that need to be constantly renewed. It is important to have a sense of purpose and a pattern to our living because baptism is our statement of service to others for the sake of the kingdom of God. Our call is to go about as an encouraging presence doing good in our own sphere of living and making the world a better place by reaching out to the excluded, the oppressed, the poor, the sick, and the lonely. What we receive as a gift is meant to be shared with others.

Jesus told us that if we follow in his footsteps we will not walk in darkness but will have the light of life. One of the graces we receive from the sacrament of baptism is the courage to face up to the challenges we meet on our pilgrim way. There is so much we can do to make Christ believable in simple ordinary ways. At the start of another year in the once made journey we can renew our own commitment to Christ and review the elements of our saving service to others. This feast is a powerful reminder of the way of life to which we have been called in baptism. It should remind us of our own baptism in consecrated waters and of the coming of the Holy Spirit that cleansed our soul from the stain of sin. We are invited to follow the Lord with enthusiasm and faith and to say no to a life of selfishness by taking on a life of love. This is an occasion to express our gratitude and appreciation for our new life as adopted children of God. Let us be thankful for all those who have shared their faith with us and have helped us to know how precious we are in God's sight.

Prayer of the Faithful

Celebrant: We turn in prayer to the Father who, by our baptism, has made us his children and present our petitions with confidence.

1. That all who administer the sacrament of baptism may receive the guidance of the Holy Spirit and proclaim without fear that Jesus is Lord.
   Lord, hear us.

2. For all who have been baptised that their lives may always bear witness to the Lord.
   Lord, hear us.

3. We pray for those who have never known Christ, that the Holy Spirit may open their minds and hearts.
   Lord, hear us.

4. May the sick and the housebound experience the Lord's healing from the tenderness and patience of those who care for them.
   Lord, hear us.

5. For those who have died that they may come to the fullness of life promised them in baptism.
   Lord, hear us.

Heavenly Father, you so loved the world that you sent your only Son to save us. Thank you for making us your children through Jesus Christ our Lord. Amen.

First Sunday in Lent

First Reading: Genesis 2:7-9, 3:1-7; Second Reading: Romans 5:12-19
Gospel: Matthew 4:1-11

The forty days of Lent put us in touch with that decisive turning point in the life of Jesus when he was called from his work as a tradesman in Nazareth, to begin the adventure of his public ministry of preaching and teaching. At the outset of his mission, led by the Spirit, he went into the desert on his own to fast, to reflect on the word of God in his life and to pray. In the wilderness there were no distractions apart from the long dark nights and the sweltering hot days during which he struggled with his ministry. He needed to be alone yet he was not lonely because he carried within himself that special relationship with God the Father.

At the opportune moment when Jesus was famished with hunger and his physical strength was at its weakest, Satan arrived on the scene to tempt him with the deceptive package of lust, prestige and power. His initial plan was to fool Jesus into breaking his fast and to get him to resort to the miraculous by changing stones into bread. When this failed, the evil schemer suggested prestige and popularity with a bout of the spectacular from the pinnacle of the temple. The final temptation was to put his trust in worldly possessions and power. All were rejected and Satan departed.

As we begin our Lenten journey we are invited to acknowledge honestly and realistically our fundamental human weakness. The readings focus on the reality of temptation and sin in the world and in our lives. Nobody likes to dwell on sin as it touches a raw nerve, especially in the light of the havoc that it has created both in society and in our individual lives. However it began, sin is a tragedy and is humanity's undoing as it has put us out of step with God's plan of things. Nowadays sin is seldom mentioned and when confronted with persistent temptation in our lives the easy option is to give in because immediate and instant gratification is the order of the day. Resisting temptation requires effort, discipline and pain on our part and there are no short cuts, or easy options in dealing with it. That is why it is comforting to know that the battle against evil was never over for Jesus any more than it is for us. The temptations that he experienced were an aspect of his human nature and he was put to the test in the same way as we are. We might not be tempted in such a dramatic fashion, but a series of small ongoing temptations not dealt with properly can result in us selling ourselves short and in settling for less than our real selves. The end result is our failure to measure up and be the person that God wants us to be.

The church is a community of sinners engaged in the battle between flesh and spirit, good and evil. We experience weakness and failure in moments of temptation especially when we place our self-interest before the worship of God and the care of others. Lent is an inward journey to that quiet inner centre of our soul where one's own life and spirit are united with the life and Spirit of God. It is a long and arduous pilgrimage of self-discovery calling us to face up to our personal weaknesses and to the distractions that so preoccupy us that we forget about God. The holy season of Lent is a time for conversion, for having a change of heart and for making an awareness of God's presence the most important reality in our lives and in our dealings with one another. We are invited to look at our own sinfulness, to fast and abstain from what we really enjoy, to give alms from what we have got and not just from what is left over and to do it for the sake of the people who have nothing. Above all we are to pray and reflect on the word of God. Lent's challenge is to take charge of our lives in ways that will set us free to live life more generously and become more Christ-like people, living in peace and harmony with one another. Our annual Lenten preparation for Easter affords us the opportunity to take time to discover where we are on our journey, clear our lives of clutter and in the vast open spaces of the desert to regain our spiritual bearings and experience God's presence.

Prayer of the Faithful

Celebrant: As we begin our Lenten journey we turn to God the Father who knows our needs and ask his help in preparing for a worthy celebration of Easter.

1. That our Holy Father may be graced with the insight and strength to carry out his authority and responsibility for the good of the church.
   Lord, hear us.

2. May all members of the church grow in faith this Lenten season through prayer, fasting and almsgiving.
   Lord, hear us.

3. That each of us may experience true reconciliation and renewal during this time of grace.
   Lord, hear us.

4. We pray for families torn apart by unresolved hurts and misunderstandings. May God's grace help them to become reconciled with one another.
   Lord, hear us.

5. That those members of our community who have died recently may share freely in the life of God
   Lord, hear us.

Heavenly Father, your Son was tempted as we are. Support us in time of temptation, give us strength in our weakness and help us to do your will in all things. We make our prayer through Christ, our Lord. Amen.

Second Sunday in Lent
First Reading: Genesis 12:1-4; Second Reading: 2 Timothy 1:8-10
Gospel: Matthew 17:1-9

The transfiguration scene, packed with awesome majesty and mystery, captures our imagination. Little did Peter, James and John realise on accepting the invitation of Jesus to climb up a mountainside, that they would experience one of the most memorable events in their lives. They had been companions of Jesus for more than a year and although his preaching, teaching and miracles had been sensational, they had noted nothing different in his physical appearance to distinguish him from other people. On the mountain, as Christ was absorbed prayerfully in God the Father's presence, all that changed. For a few shining moments, bathed in blinding brilliance, his countenance was altered as he shed his human appearance. Enveloped in a strong and dazzling light, his divinity flashed forth. What the apostles witnessed was an experience out of this world. At that incredible moment they saw that Jesus was not just a great man but the Messiah who had been promised for centuries. Shielding their eyes from the splendour of the light, the apostles were filled with fear as the voice of the Almighty echoed from the clouds 'This is my Son the beloved, he enjoys my favour. Listen to him.' The moment of glory was short lived and the apostles were back down the mountain to the problems of ordinary life.

It is said that God the Father momentarily lifted the curtain and revealed the true glory of his Son in order to strengthen Peter, James and John against the horror and humiliation of the garden of Gethsemane where they would see Christ reduced to utter misery. This vision was to strengthen them against losing hope and caving in to despair at the arrival of that dreaded hour when they would see Jesus suffer and die. The wonder and awe and the grace of that deeply mystical experience on the mountaintop would prepare them for the hardship of Calvary and the humiliation of the cross.

From our own experience of travelling on life's journey, we can identify with the plight of Abraham. In his old age he was called by God to cut his family roots, leave behind all that was dear to him and set out on a journey with nothing but the assurance of a blessing. Abraham believed enough to risk his future and to rely on God's promise. As pilgrims on the move we have little idea of what God has in store for us. His promise is that at journey's end we will all be transfigured, see him as he really is and share in the vision of his glory. In the meantime the important thing is to remain willing spirits, open to God's influence and ready to venture forth along unknown paths. Our eagerness to step out in faith will transform the landscape of our lives. Only by living as God wants us to live can we reach our full potential and achieve the happiness he has planned for us.

During Lent, as we journey with Jesus towards his passion, death and resurrection, we have an opportunity to examine our lives and the quality of our witness to his teaching. We are challenged to move away from where we have grown comfortable. Once we let go of our cherished belongings we become freer and lighter and are capable of following Christ more closely. The transfiguration is not a once off happening that took place on a mountaintop some two thousand years ago. God is always passing by and Christ still walks among us but in our hurry we never even notice. Our journey through life is invariably a series of peaks and valleys, heights and hollows, ups and downs. On the pilgrim way we come to realise our own times of special grace which put us in touch with the mystery of God. It may be the love of newly weds pronouncing their vows, the magnificence of a sunset, a walk by the riverbank. Whatever it is that gives us an experience of something beyond ourselves that can be described as a brush with the holy or an encounter with God, is a grace-filled moment, to be savoured. Sometimes the holiness of God breaks through into our lives with a piece of good news when we are down on our luck or a kind act that restores our faith in human nature. Our own moments of special light offer us insight into the future and give us courage and perseverance to continue and to travel hopefully in days of darkness when we are overcome by our own personal weakness. The Transfiguration is a glimpse of the glorious future, which awaits us all.

Prayer of the Faithful

Celebrant: With confidence in God the Father who has promised us a glorified life in the image of his Son, we make our prayer.

1. That our Holy Father and all the clergy may courageously lead their people as they preach the nearness of God's kingdom.
   Lord, hear us.

2. That each of us may experience a spiritual renewal and conversion of heart during this Lenten season.
   Lord, hear us.

3. We pray for those who are earnestly searching for the truth. May they discover guidance in Jesus who is a light shining in the darkness.
   Lord, hear us.

4. For the elderly, sick and the housebound. May they always be treated with the dignity and respect due them as children of God.
   Lord, hear us.

5. We pray for those who have died. May the kingdom of heaven with all its joys be their eternal home.
   Lord, hear us.

Heavenly Father, enlighten our darkness, show us the path that leads to eternal life. May we never fail to take up the cross which comes to us in so many ways. We make our prayer through Christ, our Lord. Amen.

Third Sunday in Lent

First Reading: Exodus 17:3-7; Second Reading: Romans 5:1-2, 5-8
Gospel: John 4:5-42

Lent is a wonderful time for gospel stories and today is no exception. The scene is set with the arrival of Jesus at Jacob's well, a familiar stopping place used by travellers passing through Samaria. This was a stretch of land in the middle of Palestine where Jews did not feel at all comfortable. Weary after trudging along for hours on dusty roads in the midday heat, he sat down for a rest. When a Samaritan woman came to draw water Jesus broke every rule of social convention by striking up a conversation with her and asking for a drink to quench his thirst. She knew from his accent that he was a Jew and was taken aback by the directness of his request. After all, Jews and Samaritans did not speak because of centuries of embittered and deep-rooted hatred, which was smouldering below the surface. At first the woman appeared to have no time for him and his simple request for water was met with a curt reply. 'Why are you, a Jew asking me, a Samaritan for a drink?' Without losing his composure Jesus continued the conversation, absorbed the woman's anger and made the startling statement that he could provide her with living water, which would quench her thirst for all time. The very thought of never having to go back to the well ever again was so amazing that it appealed to her immediately and she was instantly interested in his offer. There was clearly a misunderstanding here because the woman did not fully comprehend his meaning. She was thinking in terms of quenching human thirst with fresh spring water from the bottom of the well while Jesus was referring to the deep spiritual thirst within the human heart, craving for fulfilment which could only be quenched and satisfied by the living waters of grace.

Recognising Jesus as a man of extraordinary spiritual insight she listened attentively and drew comfort from his every word. His conversation gradually lead the woman to realise that there was a spiritual thirst deep within us that could never be quenched with water and that hankering after material things only aggravated and increased this spiritual thirst. He encouraged her to reflect on the significant events of her own life and she unburdened her soul. This helped her to get in touch with her inner emptiness of spirit, which was the cause of a deep distress. With the break up of five marriages behind her and happiness as elusive as ever, she clearly realised that her life was in a mess and that she was severely hurt inside. Aware of her sinfulness, she came to a clearer understanding of what she was thirsting for and was anxious to break the cycle of sin, shame and separation. Hers was the deepest thirst of the human heart. She was thirsting for God, seeking his forgiveness and longing for his presence. To this woman, desperately searching for happiness, Christ restored a sense of dignity and worth by releasing her from her guilt and offering her nothing less than a share in the spirit of God leading to eternal life. Once confirmed in faith, the woman's conversion was so amazing that she set off for the town, unstoppable with excitement, to spread the good news among her friends and bring others to Christ.

We can all learn a lesson from the Samaritan woman, who was no saint by any earthly standards, but was sincere and honest of heart in telling her story. As we journey through life in our search for complete happiness and for total love, we can drink at the wells of power, pleasure and prestige only to discover that there still remains a gnawing uneasiness. Trying to quench a spiritual thirst with material things is like trying to satisfy a physical thirst with salt water. The more we drink, the thirstier we become. The truth is that we are all empty vessels and only capable of being fulfilled with something spiritual. When we enter into the depths of our heart, we find that there is a tremendous desire, an inner ache within us that only the love of God can satisfy. It is part of our make-up to crave for the unending, the unchanging and the eternal. If we remain true to our baptismal calling, Christ will quench our spiritual thirst with the living water of grace, which will lead us to eternal life. The Samaritan woman gives us great hope and encouragement in the way she opened her life to the saving power of Christ. Her past does not prevent her from being a messenger of the gospel.

Prayer of the Faithful

Celebrant: Gathered together as a worshipping community, we acknowledge our inner thirst for the things of the spirit and pray with confidence to God the Father who alone can quench that thirst.

1. We pray for Our Holy Father and the bishops of the church. May they be effective witnesses to the faith they profess so that all people may come to recognise Jesus as their Saviour.
   Lord, hear us.

2. We pray for young people who have wandered away from God in the pursuit of earthly happiness. May they realise that all the pleasures of the world cannot satisfy the thirst God has put within the human heart.
   Lord, hear us.

3. We pray for all who have been embittered by life. May they discover healing and peace through the support of family and friends.
   Lord, hear us.

4. We pray for doctors, nurses and those in the caring professions who use their gifts to bring Christ's love to the old, the sick and the housebound.
   Lord, hear us.

5. Welcome into your eternal home our departed relatives and friends.
   Lord, hear us.

Heavenly Father, help us in our weakness to repent, to reject sin and return to you with a renewed faith. We ask this through Christ our Lord Amen.

Fourth Sunday in Lent
First Reading: 1 Samuel 16:1, 6-7, 10-13
Second Reading: Ephesians 5:8-14; Gospel: John 9: 1-41

It is difficult for us to imagine what it is like to be blind and to live in an isolated world of overpowering darkness, groping one's way through life without an idea of what colour means or a human face looks like. The joy, the wonder, the awe and the reverence which nature in its many aspects can evoke, are entirely missing. This gospel story featuring a blind man who had been doomed to darkness since the day of his birth is one of the most spectacular miracles of its kind in the New Testament. We don't even know the blind man's name but until his encounter with Jesus he was reduced to a monotonous life of poverty. Sitting daily in the same spot he pleaded for alms and stretched out his hand for bread whenever the sound of passing footsteps reached his ears.

We can picture the pure joy he felt at seeing colour and shape and becoming aware of human behaviour for the first time. These were fascinating and surprising discoveries. We can visualise him leaping with excitement and rushing back through the streets to tell his family the news of his cure. Little did he realise that the restoration of his sight would put him on a collision course with the religious authorities and get him into trouble. The establishment was out to give him a grilling as to the source of his cure. They tried to browbeat him into denying that Jesus healed him, but to no avail. His gratitude was boundless and during the uproar that followed, the beggar kept his cool. The more the Pharisees badgered him as to the source of his cure, the more courageous he became in affirming that it was Jesus who gave him sight and brought him into the light of day. Healed of his physical blindness, the man's mind and heart were gradually opened to the power of God at work in his life. Now that he had learned to see in the fullest sense he became intensely aware of how the Pharisees were spiritually blind in their wilful refusal to believe Christ. Their religious system had the measure of God and they pointed to the violation of the Sabbath Day as clear proof that the healing was not the work of God. We must all beware of becoming as blind as they were, otherwise we will miss so much of what is good and true and beautiful.

Spiritual blindness is common in every generation and there are none so blind as those who do not wish to see. Often in daily conversation when admitting to mistakes we say phrases like … 'It suddenly dawned on me' … 'I was completely in the dark' … 'How blind I was' … 'Now, I see!' We can be so wrapped up in our plans and agendas, our biases and prejudices that we lose the sensitivity to really see. As a result we only see what suits us and disregard the rest. In doing so we develop blind spots and lose out on the richness and blessing of the ordinary. The darkness is around us and within us when the window of our soul is closed to the needs of others, or when our vision is limited by jealousy, clouded by hatred and distorted by political, religious or racial bigotry. Deep down in all of us there are shadowy corners where mysterious depths of pride, falseness and lust abound. We remain in the dark until we come in faith to see who Jesus really is. To know him is to see things differently and to begin to live in the light.

Lent is a reminder that we are to cast aside the shameful deeds of darkness and to walk in the light of Christ by living in complete goodness, uprightness and truth. We are made for glory and the purpose of our existence is union with God. Every step of our pilgrimage is a journey of faith, discovery and understanding, leading us to the fullness of that light. Jesus has made us sharers in his life-giving work and we are presented with daily opportunities of radiating this light in acts of acceptance, tolerance and love. There are a huge number of charitable works that can be carried out within our immediate reach, which can help the homeless seeking shelter, the hungry begging for food and the lonely hoping for recognition. We are to rise up, overcome our spiritual blindness, put the darkness of sin behind us and live in the light of Christ.

Prayer of the Faithful

Celebrant: We turn now in prayer to God the Father and ask him to cure us of our many forms of blindness, so that we may lead lives befitting children of the light.

1. For bishops and priests who preach and teach the message of the gospels, that their gift of ministry will draw more people to seek knowledge of God.
    Lord, hear us.

2. Let us pray for all those who have lost their way in life and are living in the darkness of despair. We pray that they may come to see the light of God in the person of Jesus.
    Lord, hear us.

3. That we may never be so wrapped up in our plans and agendas that we lose the sensitivity to see the needs of those around us.
    Lord, hear us.

4. We pray for all mothers. We thank them for the gift of life, the love they have given us and the faith they have shared with us.
    Lord, hear us.

5. For those who have died recently. Grant them eternal rest and perpetual light.
    Lord, hear us.

Heavenly Father, you have loved us, even when we have turned away from you in our sinfulness. Grant us the grace to live in the light of your truth. We ask this through Christ, our Lord. Amen.

Fifth Sunday in Lent

First Reading: Ezekiel 37:12-14; Second Reading: Romans 8:8-11
Gospel: John 11:1-45

We have all been let down at one time or another by friends, so we can readily understand the disappointment of Martha and Mary when Jesus, who was their close family friend, failed to turn up at the sick bed of their brother. He did not even come for the burial. Martha was annoyed at his absence and her reproach was straight from the heart when she said, 'If you had been here, my brother would not have died.' Nevertheless, his presence had a calming effect and he was quickly immersed in this sad scene of grief and loss. At the sight of Mary in tears, he was troubled and wept. He was broken hearted at the loss of a friend and was not ashamed to display his feelings.

This gospel passage is a drama with constant motion. We watch Christ consoling the sisters, proceeding in their company to their brother's grave, and giving orders for the stone covering the entrance to be rolled back. Then, to their utter astonishment, he commands Lazarus to come out of the tomb. We can imagine the tears of surprised joy streaming down the cheeks of Martha and Mary as they once more embrace their brother Lazarus. They had never for one moment doubted that Jesus' power over life and death was absolute.

This miracle is not just about Jesus performing the impossible by bringing a man back to physical life. That is a short-term benefit as Lazarus is restored to earthly life only to die again some years later. The real focus is on belief. It is an attempt by Jesus to lift up Martha and Mary's awareness as to who he really is and what life in him signifies. This raising of Lazarus had a deeper meaning, indicating Jesus as the life-giving word of God and the onlookers did not miss the point. Religious leaders were angry because as a result of this cure people turned their attention to Jesus and were inclined to listen to his teaching.

The seed of this new life was planted in each of us at baptism and was the beginning of our sharing in God's grace. It is gradually deepened through the action of the Holy Spirit but it depends on our sincere and generous co-operation. However without our continued efforts the life we received in the sacrament can weaken and fade and we become dead to the voice of Christ calling us to himself.

As Lent approaches its climax we are being challenged to renew our baptismal calling by rooting out those obstacles that stand between God and us, so that we can walk refreshed into the new life of Easter. When we make a conscious decision to live a life of committed service to God, we have to let many things die in our old lives, which are selfish and incompatible with the gospel message. Being a good Christian means dying to self. This is a difficult challenge as we are part of a society that promotes self-interest and encourages us to be self-assertive. The pressures encouraging selfishness are stronger than ever. We are plagued with advertisements persuading us to spoil ourselves, pamper our children and be self-indulgent. We aren't even shocked anymore when we read about mothers walking out on their family to pursue their own happiness. How often do we hear the remark: 'It's my life and I have to do what suits me best.' The perception is that this life is all that there is and that death is the end, so make the most of it. This gospel questions such thinking, which is not the way Christ taught us to search for happiness. He states that without the Spirit there is a total absence of life, and stresses the importance of genuinely getting to know oneself in order to die daily to sin and selfishness. Each time we overcome our selfishness we are sharing in the newness of life Christ has come to bring,

This morning, the Lord is standing at the door of our hearts, seeking an entrance and waiting for us to roll back those boulders which have kept us locked up in a shadowy existence. Christ wants to enter and bring his life-giving presence to those places of darkness, shame and even death. The good news is that he sets free those who are bound by sin and can bring back people to life no matter how long they have been dead to the things of the spirit. He is calling us to face the shadows, to come into the sunshine and walk in the fullness of life.

Prayer of the Faithful

Celebrant: We turn now in prayer to the Father who, through the life, death and resurrection of his Son, Jesus Christ, has brought us back to the life of friendship with him and make our requests.

1. Let us pray for Our Holy Father and the bishops of the church. May they be faithful servants giving encouragement to all God's people.
   Lord, hear us.

2. That our lives may bear witness to the compassion and goodness of the Lord.
   Lord, hear us.

3. That as we make this Lenten journey we may become more generous in sharing our resources.
   Lord, hear us.

4. For those who have lost someone dear to them, that their hope in Christ may give them strength.
   Lord, hear us.

5. We pray for the dead. May they share in the company of Jesus who is the Resurrection and the Life.
   Lord, hear us.

Heavenly Father, you planted within our hearts the hope of eternal life. Bring us and all those we love to the fullness of that new life of grace. We make our prayer through Christ, our Lord. Amen.

Palm Sunday
First Reading: Isaiah 50:4-7; Second Reading: Philippians 2:6-11
Gospel: Matthew chapters 26 and 27

We gather in this momentous week of the church's calendar to recall Christ's passion and to trace his lonely journey to the hill of Calvary. Palm Sunday and Christ's triumphant entry on a humble donkey into Jerusalem open the door through which we enter Holy Week. He is openly proclaimed as the Messiah by an enthusiastic throng of followers in festive mood, waving palms and carpeting his pathway with their clothing. For a short time, it seems from the popular acclamations of the crowd who are preparing to make him king, that success has finally come to his mission. However, his popularity poses a threat to authority and as the days unfold, the solemn procession and acclamation from the holiday crowd gradually turn sour and the mood changes. What follows is a travesty of justice and a connivance by authority with everything that runs counter to decent civilised human behaviour. This is a week that swings from one extreme to the other. The voices that shout Hosannas become cries of hatred and despair as Jesus exchanges his donkey ride for a nightmare trip on a wooden cross. From palm branches to passion, from hosanna to heckling, from majesty to mockery, from friend to foe, we are reminded that crowds are fickle and of the depth to which unredeemed humanity can sink.

The story of the passion speaks for itself and its presentation is simple and direct. In it we glimpse the presence of the contradictory in our lives. As we travel along the road with Jesus and encounter all the people he meets we relive the events and have an opportunity to enter into the sufferings of Christ during his last days on earth. The people involved in his death are so like us that we can identify with them. There is no role in the drama that we are not capable of playing, be it Judas betraying with a poisoned kiss, Peter denying any association or Pilate washing his hands of all responsibility. Christ's closest friends are a complete let down in this hour of crisis. There is a Judas in us all. We portray the shades of Peter when out of shame we deny friendship. Like Pilate, we have cold feet and are inclined to wash our hands of difficult situations. We would all like to be identified with those who stood their ground and faced up to reality. Veronica wiped his brow, Simon of Cyrene helped carry the cross, the women of Jerusalem shed tears by the wayside and then there was the unconditional love of his mother Mary.

There are many scenes in literature describing the inhumanity of man to man but none so poignant as the one contained in Matthew's gospel. It's an appalling spectacle. Crucifixion is one of the most lingering and torturing methods of execution ever devised. Even before it starts, his agony in the garden produces sweat like great drops of blood falling to the ground. Throughout the events of his trial and sentencing, Jesus' posture is one of silent composure and is in sharp contrast to the scheming conduct of his enemies. The passion story lays bare the forces of evil and the wickedness of sin. However, it reveals the goodness of God for what appears as the triumph of the powers of darkness at his death turns out to be the great moment of God's saving plan.

The cross, which is the undisputed symbol of the passion, stands at the centre of the Christian story and is a sign of the price paid for our shame and sinfulness. While it is an instrument of torture and execution, it is a sign of salvation and speaks of love in an atmosphere of hate. Christ died for our sins on the Hill of Calvary and calls us to follow the way of the cross. The way of suffering which is the way of love will only be fully understood in the light of eternity. We know from our experience that pain, suffering and death are part of life and that there is no escaping them. Walking with Jesus on the road to Calvary we learn the meaning of the cross –the depth of God's love for us and the effect of evil in the world. 'The way of the cross', writes Michel Quoist, 'winds through our towns and cities, our hospitals and factories, and through our battlefields ... It is in front of these stations that we must stop and meditate and pray to the suffering Christ for the strength to love him.' Lord, in this time of repentance, we call out for your mercy. Bring us back to you and to the life your Son won for us by his death on the cross.

Prayer of the Faithful

Celebrant: On this solemn day, we place all our needs before our heavenly Father and ask him to deepen our faith, so that we can come to a greater understanding of the passion and death of his Son.

1. We pray that the church throughout the world may be a sign of hope and a source of comfort to all those who are suffering and carrying intolerable burdens.
   Lord, hear us.

2. For our parish community that this celebration of Holy Week may draw us closer to Christ in faith, hope and love.
   Lord, hear us.

3. We pray for people who have been betrayed in life and those who suffer persecution for their faith.
   Lord, hear us.

4. That the sick and housebound may draw courage and strength from the cross of Christ.
   Lord, hear us.

5. We pray for all who have died during the past week, that the kingdom of heaven with all its joys will be theirs.
   Lord, hear us.

Heavenly Father, as we begin this week of grace, help us to follow in the footsteps of your Son and keep us mindful of his boundless love. We ask this through Christ, our Lord. Amen.

Easter Sunday

First Reading: Acts 10:34, 37-43; Second Reading: Colossians 3:1-4
Gospel: John 20:1-9

Easter is very much in keeping with the mystery of newness of life, which comes in the springtime of the year. An atmosphere of freshness radiates on this Easter morning as the church joyfully proclaims the good news that Jesus has broken the chains of death and has risen triumphant from the grave. The dawn is breaking over the hills of Palestine as the grief stricken women make their way to the tomb to anoint the body with spices. We can sense their shock and surprise on seeing the stone rolled back, the guards stretched out, the body missing and an angel greeting them with the news that he is not here, he has risen. Their arrival at the burial site brings them to the threshold of an experience with undreamt of possibilities that they would never have dared to imagine. The women are the first messengers of Christ's resurrection. Their hearts are filled with the wonder and excitement at the event as they hasten to tell disciples of the extraordinary happening. Before very long the whole community is buzzing with the news that Jesus has risen from the dead and that his life has ended in victory and not in defeat. Nothing will ever be the same again.

We live in an imperfect world of unattained ideals and broken promises and we feel fenced in by evil and crushed by personal sinfulness. Yet, in spite of our frustrated hopes, there is something within us that yearns for the best, that longs for true freedom, real happiness and lasting peace. We want to be assured that there is a meaning to life, a reason for our existence and a purpose to the pain and suffering we have to endure. The resurrection which is at the heart of the Christian faith provides answers to our questioning. It announces to a tormented world that God absorbs all human sin and defeats it with love. Christ's rising from the dead proclaims that Calvary was not just a hill where a life full of promise was ended by violent men. It was Christ's altar of sacrifice where he offered his life for the sins of humankind. God who created us has no intention of standing idly by to watch us self-destruct. We have a destiny to fulfil and as a resurrection people we are invited to open ourselves to the Easter life that God offers us with all its hopes and possibilities. The Easter message has no relevance or meaning if Christ has not risen from the dead and our hearts are still in bondage because we are still locked in the tombs of our own sinfulness. Rolling away the stones that imprison us so that we can come forth bright and powerful into the light of the risen Christ, involves an effort on our part. It means committing anew the bits and pieces of our fragmented lives to the vision Christ has opened up for us. We are called to proclaim the good news that the deepest truth is to be found in hope and not in despair, in life not in death, and that light will triumph over darkness. Once we carry the spirit of Easter in our hearts, we add an extra dimension to our humdrum lives.

The whole mystery of Easter is about the overwhelming love of God being offered to every person. All peoples are God's concern and come under his care. Everyone without exception has access to God's forgiveness in Jesus' name. There is eternal life for all who come to him. We are the communicators of this joyful message, which is much in keeping with the mystery of new life bursting out in the springtime of the year. The job in hand is to announce to those who are in the darkness of despair that there is a dawn of hope. Our belief in the God who makes all things new must influence our whole lives and show itself in the way we treat one another, our family and friends and people who are unknown to us. We are present in the world in a new way when we affirm life, thirst for justice and strive for peace. Easter encourages us to set our hearts on what is above and not to neglect the deep realities by which alone we truly live. On this Easter Day we pray God to let joy fill our hearts and to give us the grace to bear witness to the resurrection which brings new life to the world.

Prayer of the Faithful

Celebrant: On this glorious day (night) when Jesus Christ rose from the dead and restored our life of grace, we turn to God the Father in prayer and ask for all our needs.

1. We pray that the church may be renewed in the risen Christ and bring his message of hope and love to all the world.
   Lord, hear us.

2. We pray that our parish community may experience the joy of the resurrection in the happiness shared with others.
   Lord, hear us.

3. For all the newly baptised. May they grow in the love and the light of Christ.
   Lord, hear us.

4. That those who live with terminal illness may experience compassion and encouragement in their caregivers.
   Lord, hear us.

5. For all the faithful departed who have died to this life since our last celebration of Easter, may they be at peace in the promise of new life in the glory of God.
   Lord, hear us.

Father in heaven, hear the prayers we offer with sincere hearts. Increase our belief in the resurrection of your Son so that the joy of Easter may be with us always. We ask this through Jesus Christ, our Lord. Amen.

Second Sunday after Easter
First Reading: Acts 2: 42-47; Second Reading: 1 Peter 1: 3-9
Gospel: John 20:19-31

The apostles in the upper room were huddled in grief behind closed doors in a hopelessly desperate situation. They had gone into hiding for fear of reprisals, because the world of their dreams had literally collapsed when Jesus, their leader, had been rudely snatched from them and crucified. Gone were the exciting days of cures and miracles, when to be in the company of Jesus was an honour and a privilege. Now everything was despair and disgrace. This situation was changed dramatically when on the evening of the first day of the week Jesus, undeterred by locked doors, was standing in their midst. Their doubts were dissolved when he established his identity by showing the wounds of his passion. After greeting the apostles with his gift of peace, he poured his spirit upon them with the commission to go out and continue his saving work.

Thomas missed the moment of drama and, arriving on the scene some time later, was not at all impressed by what his companions told him. He refused to accept the word of the community that Jesus had appeared in their midst. Thomas had difficulty in believing and insisted that he must see for himself. In his denial he was intolerant and aggressive and stipulated the kind of proof he needed. Nothing less than putting his hands into the wounds would suffice: 'Unless I see the holes that the nails made in his hands and can put my finger into the holes they made, and unless I can put my hand into his side, I refuse to believe.' It was eight days later when, in the presence of Thomas, Jesus stood among the group. He greeted all but spoke only to Thomas inviting him to finger his wounds and witness for himself. Thomas saw the hallmarks of Jesus' death and came face to face with the absolute truth of God in human form. His profession of faith was in no uncertain terms the most profound and explicit voiced by any of the witnesses of the resurrection. It brings John's gospel to a triumphant conclusion.

We would be making a big mistake in dismissing Thomas as a man of little faith simply because he was disheartened, disillusioned and despairing after witnessing the death of the

Lord. There are shades of Thomas in all of us and we can identify with him amidst our own personal doubts and heart-searching questioning. In moments of crisis when the going gets tough many of us find it difficult to see beyond the surface of things. Thomas assures us that an open and enquiring mind can lead to a deeper knowledge of the truth. His doubts were those of a person who was well on the road to faith but searching. There is nothing shameful in demanding an explanation as many great insights have resulted from questioning the received wisdom of the times. The church needs to air doubts and to let it be known that there is nothing harmful when confusions and uncertainties surface. The expression of doubt and the questioning of God are important aspects of the Bible. There is plenty of doubting in the psalms, 'How long, O Lord, will you forget me? (Psalm 13:1) and lots of questioning from the prophets, 'Why did I come from the womb to see only sorrow and toil and to end my days in shame?' (Jeremiah 20:18). Nothing isolates us more than fear and uncertainty. We all know that when tragedy arrives at our doorstep and life hurts, glib answers are not helpful.

The Thomas episode in the gospel challenges us to confront our fears and to let the Risen Christ take root in our hearts. The joy, the happiness and the contentment that Christ shares with us is something inward and involves being at peace with ourselves, and in harmony with the community. This is deeper than any superficial or surface emotion. In a world of selfishness and greed we proclaim the resurrection by reaching out in service to the disadvantaged in our midst. Christ has the power to enter the doors of our hearts in the way he entered the Upper Room long ago. The experience of the Risen Christ is to be found in the community that shares his love. It is evident in the way we visit our sick, support our aged and comfort the bereaved in their grief and loss. Through the Easter mysteries God has given us birth in a new way of life, with the grace and power of his Son at work within us. Today is an occasion to express our gratitude to God for the heavenly inheritance, which is ours, and to recommit ourselves to each other as an Easter people.

Prayer of the Faithful

Celebrant: Gathered together as God's people, with confidence we pray to the Father for an increase in faith and seek his help in our struggle with doubt.

1. We pray that the church may be of one voice pointing to Christ as the source of life and happiness.
    Lord, hear us.

2. We pray for the grace of faith for those people who are groping in darkness and who are searching for meaning in their lives.
    Lord, hear us.

3. That those who live without hope may be uplifted by the events of Easter and strengthened by its message for humankind.
    Lord, hear us.

4. For the sick of our community that they may be comforted in their suffering by the care of those who tend to their needs.
    Lord, hear us.

5. For those who have died in Christ; that they may receive the fullness of eternal life promised by Jesus to all who believe in his word.
    Lord, hear us.

Heavenly Father, listen to our call for help. May we never be discouraged by our weakness as we live in the hope and trust that you are always with us. We ask this through Christ, our Lord. Amen.

Third Sunday after Easter

First Reading: Acts 2: 14, 22-33; Second Reading: 1 Peter 1:17-21
Gospel: Luke 24:13-35

This wonderful and powerful post resurrection story, which at first sight appears to be simple, continues the theme of journeying in faith. The faith of Cleopas and his friend was at a low ebb because of the death of Jesus, on whom they had pinned all their hopes and expectations. Their dreams had been dashed and they were feeling totally disillusioned and dejected. Fearful of what might happen to them if they stayed in Jerusalem, they set off on the road to Emmaus with heavy hearts. They were deep in conversation trying to make sense of the traumatic events that had happened over the previous days, when a stranger joined their company. Something in his manner prompted them to pour out the great sorrow that was troubling their hearts. They told the story of the violent events that had taken place during the Passover and how the prophet whom they believed to be the Messiah was crucified. The latest reports from some of the other disciples were of the tomb being empty and the body missing. They had placed all their trust in this man as 'The one to set Israel free', and now they were left with shattered dreams. With sympathetic love the stranger listened to their fears, opened their minds and graciously explained from the scriptures the real significance of what had happened and how it all fitted together as part of God's plan. Their faith began to grow as he explained to them about his suffering, death and rising again. 'The Messiah had to suffer in order to enter into his glory.' Nightfall was nearing but, fascinated by the stranger's conversation and eager to hear him out, they invited him to be their guest, share their hospitality and stay with them at the local inn. During the meal, as the bread was being broken, their memories were suddenly jolted, their eyes opened and they recognised Jesus. In this blessed moment of the breaking of bread they came to realise that it was the Lord of Easter in their midst, who had walked beside them on their journey, touched their hearts and opened their eyes to the inner message of the scriptures. Late though it was, they hurried back to Jerusalem to spread the good news.

Whether we like it or not, there are occasions during life when all of us are on the road to Emmaus, trying to avoid the harsh realities of daily living. In doing so we are turning our backs on our personal Jerusalem by walking away from our problems. This can happen when the little world we have fashioned, to our way of thinking, has collapsed. We have desperately tried to avoid some particular hardship but disaster strikes and we can no longer cope. Our hope had been that things would have turned out differently. Now we are left feeling abandoned, are unable to take anymore and want to run away. Life is difficult when amidst disappointments we become bewildered, despondent and uncertain. The road to Emmaus is the story of every pilgrim with an inner emptiness that only God can replenish. We just do not know how or when the Lord may make his presence felt in our lives. God may come to us on the road on which we are travelling, in the guise of a friend whose heart goes out to us in our trouble, who listens to our story, absorbs our sorrow and helps us see a glimmer of light in the midst of our darkness. While we may not recognise the Lord, he meets us wherever we happen to be. A prayerful listening to his word in scripture may help us understand the pain of some personal experience as part of God's plan for us. His word can change our whole way of looking at events and encourage us to start thinking about spiritual matters. What the word of God opens up for us is further enhanced, by our taking part in the breaking and blessing and distribution of bread at the gathering of the faithful during Mass. Every Sunday, as life's needy travellers, we assemble in community with our faults, failures and doubts to receive food for the journey which empowers us to go out and proclaim that the Lord has risen. It is during our pilgrimage with our problems and fears that we encounter the Lord who will open our eyes and enflame our hearts. We need to travel to Emmaus to realise that despite our tears, disappointments and trials there is always new hope and a reason to be at peace.

Prayer of the Faithful

Celebrant: Recalling how the disciples on the road to Emmaus recognised Christ in the breaking of bread, we pray to God the Father for a deeper appreciation of the Risen Lord as our spiritual food for the journey through life.

1. We pray for our Holy Father and the bishops of the church. May they live lives worthy of their calling.
   Lord, hear us.

2. That our parish community may never take for granted the grace we receive in our eucharistic celebration.
   Lord, hear us.

3. That the Christian witness of our lives may bring hope and light to those who are disillusioned and in the darkness of despair.
   Lord, hear us.

4. That those who are suffering may experience the healing presence of God in their pain and distress.
   Lord, hear us.

5. For those who have died in Christ: that they may enjoy the fullness of life in the company of the Risen Christ.
   Lord, hear us.

Heavenly Father, grant us the deep faith necessary to recognise your Son in all the situations in life. We make our prayer through Christ, our Lord. Amen

Fourth Sunday after Easter

First Reading: Acts 2:14a, 36-41; Second Reading: 1 Peter 2:20-25
Gospel: John 10:1-10

The image of the Good Shepherd has, from the earliest time, been woven into the language and imagery of the Bible. In the history of Christianity it is the most ancient and beloved symbol of our saviour. A favourite scene adorning places of worship shows the beautiful picture of Jesus as the Good Shepherd carrying home shoulder high a lost sheep, illustrating care, concern, strength and tenderness. This shepherd and sheep gospel story is a picture that appeals to every human heart. In this day and age few people can claim to have first hand experience of the difficulties and challenges which are part of a shepherd's life. His deep dedication to his flock extends even to risking his life for them. We are told that sheep are defenceless animals, prone to getting lost, renowned for straying and without the protection of a good shepherd fall easy prey to wild animals. Once they become familiar with their master's voice, they are totally dependent on him to lead them to fresh pastures and to keep them together out of harm's way at nightfall.

Jesus uses this powerfully appropriate imagery to teach us something about himself as the Good Shepherd. It demonstrates the protection he can offer us especially if we have been knocked off course, lost our way and neglected the life of the spirit. Living in a media age with all sorts of voices vying for our attention it is easy to lose our sense of direction and fall prey to ways of thinking that are not of the Lord. Even if we should lapse into sin and walk in the valley of the shadow of darkness he will not just patiently await our return but will seek us out with a love that knows no limit. As the shepherd appointed by God in charge of the flock he lets us know that he has a distinctive interest in us, that we are the objects of his special love and that he is willing to sacrifice his life for us. Our survival is based upon recognising the intimate and personal quality of his call when he beckons us by name. He teaches us the proper pathways to follow where we can confidently go through life with all its joys and sorrows and find safety, security and peace. Clinging to him is a sure guarantee that we will not go astray, as he is an ever-watchful friend and our surest guide to safety. His greatest concern is to give us the freedom to live life to the full.

By virtue of our baptism the life of God runs deep within us and makes us adopted brothers and sisters of the Good Shepherd. We are all involved in his life and have a share in his saving work. Each of us is called to be a shepherd in one way or another – as parents to children, as teachers to students, as a priest to his congregation. Responsibility for the welfare of others is something we can not avoid. We grow in the likeness of Christ when we have the courage to step out of ourselves and share our lives with those less fortunate than we are. Christ's own earthly ministry was marked by a sensitive approach to the weak and vulnerable. Every task no matter how small when done out of love is a sign of true greatness.

This is as good a day as any to reflect on how as a church going people we are responding to the voice of Christ calling us to be shepherds of his flock within the ordinary bits and pieces of our lives. We are all expected to live in love and work together to build a caring community. For many, living a good Catholic and Christian life means little more than squeezing in a one hour church obligation each Sunday morning with scant reference to personal conduct for the rest of the week, as if active faith amounts to nothing more than being lukewarm about the Christian way of life. On Easter Day when the Lord appeared to the disciples, they were filled with the spirit and became convinced Christians whose lives underwent a significant change with a lively faith and a new purpose in their being. The same is true for us. Once we call ourselves Christians, everything we do must be influenced by that decision. Our fundamental vocation is to be loving, caring people with a mind through which Christ thinks, a heart through which Christ loves, a voice through which Christ speaks and hands through which Christ helps.

Prayer of the Faithful

Celebrant: With trust and confidence we pray to God our Father and offer him the deep concerns and needs of the church and of the world.

1. We pray for our Holy Father and bishops of the church. May they be true shepherds leading their flocks to good pastures.
   Lord, hear us.

2. We pray for those who have wandered away from the paths of righteousness. May they hear the voice of the Good Shepherd calling them home.
   Lord, hear us.

3. We pray for an increase in vocations to the priesthood and religious life. May the youth of our community hear the voice of the Good Shepherd calling them to serve God's family in a special way.
   Lord, hear us.

4. We pray for the sick and the aged. May the healing tenderness of the Good Shepherd be present in the loving care from family and friends.
   Lord, hear us.

5. We pray for all our faithful departed. May they come to know the peace of their true home in heaven.
   Lord, hear us.

Father, hear our prayers and bless each one of us in the way you know best. May we follow wherever you lead us. We make our prayer through Christ, our Lord. Amen.

Fifth Sunday after Easter
First Reading: Acts 6:1-7; Second Reading: 1 Peter 2:4-9
Gospel: John 14:1-12

This gospel reading is an extract from the Last Supper conversation between Jesus and his disciples. Judas has hurriedly left
the room on his mission of betrayal. Knowing that death is about
to take him, Jesus, towards the end of the meal, announces his
imminent departure. The disciples are shocked, upset and
bewildered at the news. Everything around them is falling apart
because the man, whom they have renounced everything for
and staked their very lives upon, is bidding them farewell. No
doubt they feel devastated at the impending loss of leadership
and are fearful of what is going to happen to them. Sensing their
disquiet and the need for an explanation Jesus sets about
comforting them, soothing their fears and telling them not to be
troubled as he is going to the Father's House to prepare a place
for them. Thomas, who is still puzzled, seeks further clarification
and interrupts the flow of conversation by asking Jesus the way
to the place where he is going. We can always rely on Thomas to
probe deeply and here he is enquiring about our final destiny.

In one form or another human beings have been wrestling
with this problem from time immemorial. The response of Jesus
is one of his most startling and best-remembered statements. 'I
am the way, the truth and the life.' He speaks of himself as the
sure way to be absolutely confident of God's welcome into eternity. It is an assurance that in the middle of our trouble and our
pain there is no need to be afraid because he is there with us and
for us. The good news is that no matter who we are or what we
do we have a heavenly home, a place that will be ready once we
have completed our earthly journey. The road to God is sure
because it is Christ who leads the way, gives us safe guidance
and takes us to our destination. The place Jesus has in store for
us is our lasting home in heaven, a shelter where the homeless
will come home and where those who have lost their way will
one day find for themselves a safe haven and peace at last.

The whole of the Christian life is like a great pilgrimage to
the house of the Father. We are on a homeward journey to eternal life but we must not lose sight of the cross as the supreme act

of God's love. Although Christ said that he was the way, he made no mention of the trip home being trouble free. His pilgrimage to the Father brought him on the way of the cross from Gethsemane via the hill of Calvary to the resurrection. We live in a valley of tears and when we are baptised we are signed with the cross to teach us precisely this. All of us, from time to time, experience moments of extreme hardship when we are burdened with pain and suffering which seem beyond our ability to bear. We must believe that God is with us in our trouble. We may not see him but he is there. Life is a mystery and we seem to spend much of the time moving into the unknown and out of the unknown. God's presence in human life is often compared to a tapestry. We are on the side where all the threads look haphazard and the pattern is blurred. But from God's side, everything weaves together and is meaningful. In the meantime we need to have faith and trust. When trials and tribulations test our mettle, bring us to our knees and we feel discouraged, the consoling words of Jesus enable us to keep on hoping as we move through these most difficult situations. We find comfort and support in knowing that God does not forsake us. We are never alone.

The life revealed and promised at Easter exceeds every human hope and expectation. However lost we feel, however great the anguish we experience, however sad or fearful we are, the God of Easter says to us: 'Trust me; I am with you always.' The truth of Easter is so vast that our minds need to be stretched in order to receive it. The great truth, which fills our life with meaning, is that Christ is alive. As we make space in our busy lives and set about searching for God, we will discover to our joyous surprise that he seeks us first. Easter awakens us anew to the truth that there is a space within each of us which only God can fill.

Prayer of the Faithful

Celebrant: Trusting in his great mercy and love, we humbly pray to God the Father as a people in need.

1. For our Holy Father, our bishop and all who have been called to guide God's people. May they direct humankind to a knowledge and belief in Christ.
    Lord, hear us.

2. For this parish family, that the joy of the risen Christ may continue to stay in our hearts and be reflected in our work within the community in which we live.
    Lord, hear us.

3. Let us pray for those who have wandered away from God, that they may be touched by his grace and enlivened by his gift of life
    Lord, hear us.

4. We remember the sick of our parish. May their friends and family support them in their time of illness.
    Lord, hear us.

5. We pray for all our deceased relatives and friends who have gone before us marked with the sign of faith. May they rest in peace.
    Lord, hear us.

Heavenly Father, we are thankful for being called to new life in your Son. Grant us your guidance and protection. We make our prayer through Christ, our Lord. Amen.

Sixth Sunday after Easter

First Reading: Acts 8:5 8, 14 17; Second Reading: 1 Peter 3:15-18
Gospel: John 14:15-21

In his farewell discourse to the disciples, Christ has the gentlest way of conveying an important message. While preparing for his departure, in the intimacy of the upper room, where he is celebrating his final meal with his closest friends, he speaks in a deeply personal way. He assures them that they will not be abandoned nor left like orphans without someone to love them, care for them and guide them. They will be given a farewell present from his Father to strengthen them so that they will not be left to struggle with the Christian life all on their own. The gift to be given is the Holy Spirit, the breath of God's life, which is a divine force inspiring activity among people. The Spirit would entail a new set of values and attitudes residing in the heart and life of all believers. He promises that the Spirit will live in their innermost being and transform them into children of the Father.

It would be impossible to describe the change that came over the apostles once they received the Holy Spirit. It was an infinitely marvellous experience of the overwhelming presence and strength of God. Jesus came into their lives as never before, so that now they could go anywhere and witness for him. A new power was abroad in the world and they were filled with enthusiasm, a fresh vision of the future, and life in the spirit. As Pentecost approaches we are reminded of the extraordinary gift and the limitless power of the Holy Spirit at work in the world. The Spirit is nothing less than God himself crossing the great divide and making his dwelling place in the hearts of humankind. He comes in many forms and touches us in vastly varied ways. Provided we reach out in trust and leave ourselves open and receptive to his influence in our lives, the Holy Spirit will strengthen our hope and give our lives new direction.

On at least four occasions during the Last Supper, Christ said to his apostles, 'If you love me, you will keep my commandments.' We need no reminding that these words of Jesus are addressed to Christians of all times including ourselves. The commandments we are called to keep as an expression of our love for him are not the Ten Commandments but the command to love and imitate him in every aspect of our lives. All love that is genuine comes from God and God is to be found in every encounter where there is real love. This love is something that cannot be bought. It is a gift given to us with no strings attached. The supreme example of God's love was sending his only Son into the world to assure us that we are saved. The only condition required for receiving this gift is the undertaking to share it with others.

This is an occasion to step back and reflect on how we are living up to the faith we professed at baptism. Have we really responded to the Christian message or simply accepted Christianity as part of the culture into which we happened to be born? Is our baptism simply a ritual of the past? The Easter Season is an opportune time to do something by way of witnessing to the Risen Lord now living in our midst. Kindness is one of God's best gifts to the world. It drives gloom and darkness from souls as it brightens horizons and lessens pain. Random acts of kindness are those spontaneous gestures of deep down goodness, which we perform as the best of our humanity momentarily springs into full bloom.

This gospel calls us to be immersed in a culture of kindness and to have the living expression of God's goodness reflected in our face, eyes, smile and warm greeting. No one should ever approach us without coming away better or feeling happier. We are not to judge or condemn – but to overlook faults and to pardon. If we have hurt someone or caused them pain now is the time to repent of our wrongdoing, seek forgiveness and start again. Being compassionate and merciful means giving people not only our care but also our hearts. By extending kindness, we encourage others, build up God's kingdom, enrich community life and nurture our own souls. When life is over we will be judged upon how much we have loved. What will count is how we have cared for our family, the old, the poor, the handicapped and the marginalised. In this way, Christ's command to love takes hold and spreads within the community.

Prayer of the Faithful

Celebrant: Filled with the Good News of Easter, we pray to God the Father and ask his help in being open to the Spirit.

1. That the church may always be receptive to the promptings of the Holy Spirit and seek his guidance in their decisions and actions.
   Lord, hear us.

2. For families that are divided and suffering because of bitterness. May the Spirit of peace bring reconciliation so that wherever there is hurt there may be healing.
   Lord, hear us.

3. We pray that our homes may be places of peace and harmony, where parents seek to guide their children in the ways of truth and love.
   Lord, hear us.

4. For those preparing for examinations – guided by your spirit may they have full confidence in their ability.
   Lord, hear us.

5. That all the faithful departed may share in the resurrection in the life to come.
   Lord, hear us.

Almighty Father, bind us together as your church so that we may have the courage to live according to our convictions as followers of Christ. We make our prayer through Christ, our Lord. Amen.

The Feast of the Ascension
First Reading: Acts 1:1-11; Second Reading: Ephesians 1:17-23
Gospel: Matthew 28:16-20

Pilgrims making the journey to the Mount of Olives outside the walls of Bethany will be shown the marks of a lone footprint in the bare rock with the comment that this is the place where Jesus, surrounded by his disciples, said his earthly goodbyes before ascending into heavenly glory. There came a time when Jesus was no longer physically present with his followers. The feast of the Ascension marks the completion of his earthly mission, the final departure from his friends and his return to the mystery of his Father. Ascension is a way of saying that Jesus, no longer here in the flesh, has entered a new form of existence and is enjoying the presence of God. The disciples must have felt deep emotion and sadness of heart as their beloved master and companion who had been a central figure in their lives disappeared from their sight. They would no longer see him or experience the comforting assurance of his presence among them as before, when he walked and talked in their company. They were not saying goodbye to Jesus, because he had assured them that he would not abandon them. He was going away to prepare a place for them and at an unspecified time in the future he would return in glory. In the meantime they were presented with the challenge of a new mission as witnesses entrusted with the responsibility of making disciples of all nations and of working for the establishment of God's kingdom in the world. Their task was to show Jesus to the world and to proclaim to all peoples the salvation that he had won.

The Ascension celebrates a significant turning point in Jesus' relationship with us. He is returning to the Father so that he can be present to the church in a more accessible manner. While on earth his ministry was limited to Israel, after the ascension Christ in his glorified state has a power whose outreach is universal. The good news is that he is present in the church through the Spirit, the Lord the giver of life. What appeared as a departure was only a means to a more intimate, lengthy and universal stay with us. It is the assurance that the church will always enjoy the living presence of Jesus. At moments when we feel hopeless and abandoned, the words, 'I am with you always; yes to the end of time,' give us the consolation that Christ is still with us, watching over us, caring for us, and hoping that we do not wander out of his sight. This feast calls us to deepen our faith in the many ways that Jesus is now present among us. He speaks to us as we listen attentively to the reading of the scriptures. We are aware of his presence as we receive the Eucharist. He is alive in our hearts when we do our best through acts of charity to make his gospel real in our lives.

This is a festival of joy and hope as it focuses on heaven as our journey's end and longed-for destination. Ascension Sunday is an answer to the deep yearning within us for fulfilment and our heartfelt longing for happiness. It gives meaning to life and a purpose to our striving. We rejoice that Jesus who destroyed sin and conquered death has returned to the right hand of the Father, allowing us to get a glimpse of our future destiny. It opens our eyes to the promise that, 'Where he has gone we hope to follow', and challenges us to believe in his presence even when he seems absent.

Our best way of celebrating the ascension is to live in this passing world with our hearts set on a world that will never end. If the love of Christ is burning in our hearts we will realise the vital role we have to play in spreading the good news. Here and now we are entrusted with the task of being the visible presence of Christ's saving love in our community. We do this through the assistance we offer those thrown into despair with life's miseries by encouraging them to keep on trying and not to give up. Once his peace and his power have touched us we are on the right road to establishing a community of justice, truth and peace in our own small corner of life. The ascension announces the good news that Christ is with us always. He has not left us. He has simply taken on a new role.

Prayer of the Faithful

Celebrant: On this day of promise we place all our hopes and longing before God the Father and ask his favour.

1. We pray for our Holy Father and bishops of the church that they may grow daily in awareness of their special mission as Christ's witnesses.
   Lord, hear us.

2. We pray for ourselves as we struggle to live and spread the message of Christ and take courage from his ascension.
   Lord, hear us.

3. We pray for the gift of reconciliation between all those who are divided by prejudice or bitterness.
   Lord, hear us.

4. We pray that the Feast of the Ascension of the Lord may renew the vision of those who have lost hope and are in the darkness of despair at this time.
   Lord, hear us.

5. That our friends who were baptised in Christ and have now completed their earthly journey, may share in the power and glory of his resurrection.
   Lord, hear us.

Heavenly Father, hear our prayers spoken and unspoken. May the ascension of your Son bring us to a greater knowledge and closer following of him. We ask this through Christ our Lord. Amen.

Seventh Sunday after Easter

First reading: Acts 1:12-14; Second Reading: 1 Peter 4:13-16
Gospel: John 17:1-11

The Last Supper took place on an April evening in Jerusalem some two thousand years ago. Down the centuries artists have tried to capture the scene in the Upper Room on canvas. We can all recall pictures of Jesus presiding at table with cup in hand and the worshipful wonder on the faces of the eleven apostles as they gaze into the master's eyes. Judas Iscariot was missing for he had left the table earlier, on undisclosed business. Jesus alone was fully aware that Judas was off plotting his betrayal with the rulers of Jerusalem. John's gospel gives us a summary of the words Jesus spoke on the occasion of the Last Supper. We must keep in mind that it is only a brief account, as no memory could have recalled word for word everything Jesus said to his apostles on that solemn occasion, just before his arrest in the garden of Gethsemane. It is his farewell address to the men who had been his close companions and with whom he lived and laboured for the previous three years. During that time he had performed many marvellous works but training the apostles to take over his mission was his most important accomplishment. His earthly ministry was now drawing to a close. His hour had come and it was time to let go, to be delivered to his enemies and to hand on his mission to his disciples. Everything was about to fall apart and the drama leading to his death had just begun. With betrayal and crucifixion less than twenty-four hours away, all his concern was centred on the apostles he was leaving behind and to whom he was entrusting his gospel. His journey in the world was over and yet through his followers he would journey on. The future of God's word was in their hands. They were dreaming his dream and if they failed, his lifetime of labour to establish his church would be in vain.

There is a mystery and a beauty about the high priestly prayer of Christ as he expresses to the Father what is deepest within himself. We get the feeling that we are eavesdropping on a very intimate conversation between Jesus and the Father. It is a passionate prayer recalling his life's work and the offering of himself to the Father. The apostles must have listened attentively as he stood in their midst and made special mention of them, his chosen ones who would soon take up the challenge of spreading the good news. Knowing the difficulties they would face, he asks the Father to protect them from evil and for them to be a good influence and example to all they meet. As we listen to Christ's perfect prayer on the eve of his crucifixion, we are conscious of the imperfection of our own prayer. Most of us don't find it easy to pray. Our difficulty stems from being too busy, always in a hurry and not having time. Our lifestyles proclaim that we are more concerned with doing than being, with activity rather than reflection. Spiritual writers keep telling us that prayer is absolutely necessary if there is to be a deepening of spirituality and enrichment in our lives. It forces us to face the reality of who we are, what are we about while here on earth and where are we going? If we don't pray we will never confront ourselves with these most important questions. Prayer has become a lost treasure that helps to make sense of our lives and puts our problems in perspective.

The reading from the Acts of the Apostles makes mention of three groups of people waiting together after the Ascension of Our Lord, for the coming of the Spirit. Those disciples, who were with him on the Mount of Olives, return to the city, enter the place where they were staying and devote themselves to prayer. A chapter in the story of salvation has closed and another has not yet opened. They are a community expecting something new to happen to them and attentive to the present moment through prayer. Before they go out and proclaim the Risen Christ to the whole world, they must wait and let the word of God happen in their lives. Luke tells us that they spent their time in waiting by devoting themselves to constant prayer. Waiting which is grounded in prayer, is a necessary preparation for the spreading of the gospel. The disciples and Mary made time to pray and so must we. Without prayer our lives are impoverished.

Prayer of the Faithful

Celebrant: United with the whole church throughout the world as we wait for a fresh outpouring of the Spirit of Pentecost, we pray in trust and hope to the Father.

1. For our church leaders. that they may have the insight and courage to recognise new opportunities to bring the word of God to all people.
   Lord, hear us.

2. That all world leaders may strive daily for peace and justice by working towards an end to violence and hatred among all people.
   Lord, hear us.

3. We pray for young people who are preparing for examinations and who are waiting in hope for many things. Guided by the Spirit may they have full confidence in their ability.
   Lord, hear us.

4. May the healing power of the risen Christ touch the lives of all who suffer from illness, abuse or depression.
   Lord, hear us.

5. For those who have gone before us marked with the sign of faith. May they journey through the valley of death to resurrection.
   Lord, hear us.

Heavenly Father, help us to keep in mind that Christ our Saviour promised to remain with us to the end of time. We make our prayer through Christ, our Lord. Amen.

Pentecost Sunday
First reading: Acts 2:1-11;
Second Reading: 1 Corinthians 12:3-7, 12-13; Gospel: John 20:19-23

From the earliest of times Christians have celebrated Pentecost, the birthday of the church, as one of the principal feast days of the year. The scene was set in the Upper Room where the apostles were assembled wondering what was to become of them and praying about their uncertain future. They were anything but an impressive sight, huddled together behind locked doors for fear of the Jews. Suddenly there was a sound from heaven like the mighty roar of a powerful wind, which flung open the doors, and a bright light like flames of fire swept down upon them. As the light kept shining brighter, their faces glowed and their hearts were set on fire. The Holy Spirit descended upon them and in no time they were out on the streets announcing boldly in many languages that Jesus is Lord. Once they had experienced the joy of God breathing the kiss of life into them they were no longer lacking in confidence. The fear and confusion that had gripped their hearts gave way to courage and a bold conviction to proclaim God's liberating love. They went public and to the amazement and astonishment of the onlookers, preached fearlessly in the marketplace where the spirit of God gave them ears to hear and understand people of different cultures. The outpouring of the Holy Spirit totally transformed the apostles and changed their lives. The gift of the Spirit brought out the best in them and they were no longer humbled by their limitations or overwhelmed by their weaknesses. On that first Pentecost Day the church was born.

The action of the Holy Spirit at Pentecost was not a one-off experience at the birth of Christianity, for the same Spirit breathes life into the church in every age and continues to do so in our times. While God has sent the Holy Spirit as his first gift to those who believe, to complete his work on earth and bring us the fullness of grace, his influence is not restricted to places of worship nor confined to the hearts of good living people. Everybody has access to the Holy Spirit and that includes people who are not religious. 'The Spirit breathes where he wills.' Provided we leave ourselves open to give God room and make space for him, the Spirit will enter our being and offer us a new vision of the future.

Pentecost is a call to action. It is an invitation to do our part to spread God's kingdom on earth. The apostles, empowered by the Spirit of the Lord, show us what we can do as a believing community. The secret of receiving the Spirit is to empty ourselves of such things as pride, arrogance and self-reliance. God's blessings flow into us mainly through our poverty. If we acknowledge our helplessness, are aware of our limitations and humbly admit our sinfulness we can better direct our thoughts and feelings towards God who will make us fully alive. Once we start listening to God and invite him to enter and make his dwelling place within our hearts nothing less than a spiritual powerhouse will be at work in our lives.

At a time like the present when old structures in family and church are tumbling down many of us are trying our best to hang on to the Christian standards, customs and worship that shaped our lives in the past. Like the apostles in the Upper room we are fearful of what will happen to us. Overwhelmed by change, we wonder what the future will bring. We forget that to live is to change and to become perfect is to change often. The apostles who were waiting in prayer for the arrival of the Spirit give us comfort for we can do the same. The Spirit will become our guiding light, giving us the courage to face up to problems, helping us to discover personal resources we were unaware of and the vision to see new ways forward while contending with difficulties.

The message of Pentecost is that we are not alone. God is with us on our journey to the kingdom. At the Last Supper he promised that he would not leave his disciples desolate. He sent them the Holy Spirit on Pentecost Day. Neither will he abandon us. Today we ask God to come into our lives and to strengthen us with his Spirit so that we will be his voice where the sick need healing, the hungry need feeding and the distressed need comforting.

Prayer of the Faithful

Celebrant: As we gather for this Eucharist on the Feast of Pentecost which confirmed the apostles in their faith, we pray to the Father for the strength to witness as they did.

1. For our Holy Father and all who hold positions of responsibility in the church, that they may be ever open to the challenges of the Spirit of God and be an inspiration to all who look to them for leadership.
   Lord, hear us.

2. We pray to the Holy Spirit for the gift of patience so that we may be more tolerant of the faults of others.
   Lord, hear us.

3. We pray to the Holy Spirit that all our actions may come from a heart filled with grace.
   Lord, hear us.

4. For all who find life burdensome because of illness, poverty or sadness. May the healing power of the Holy Spirit touch their lives and ease their burdens.
   Lord, hear us.

5. We pray for all those who have gone before us. May God, through the power of the Holy Spirit, give them a share in the resurrection of his Son.
   Lord, hear us.

Heavenly Father, let this day of Pentecost be an outpouring of your Spirit to us all, that we may be a shining light amidst the darkness of the world. We make our prayer through Christ, our Lord. Amen.

Trinity Sunday
First Reading: Exodus 34:4-6, 8-9
Second reading: 2 Corinthians 13:11-13; Gospel: John 3:16-18

For many of us, long before we had our first lesson in religion, or learned to say the Our Father or recite the Hail Mary, our parents taught us how to bless ourselves and make the sign of the cross while they uttered the words, 'In the name of the Father and of the Son and of the Holy Spirit. Amen.' This distinguishing symbolic action of our faith in God being one in three persons sums up the feast we are celebrating today. It speaks to us of the unbounded mystery of God and is the rock from which we are hewn as well as being the source of our hope and joy. Our understanding of God as one in three persons came only by degrees. This was an insight into the life of God which we could never have discovered on our own, and even after having been told we still have no understanding of how this can be. Our knowledge of the Trinity surfaced from what Jesus said and did while he was here on earth when he, ever so carefully and gradually, made known his relationship to God the Father and the Holy Spirit. As long as we live in this world we will never uncover the mystery of the Trinity, even though the veil, which envelops it, is lifted ever so slightly. The little that is revealed to us is an invitation to share in the life of the Father, Son and Holy Spirit.

We are part of a culture that is not at all comfortable with mystery. Surrounded as we are by our tremendous achievements in technology, we have come to believe that there are no limits to our knowledge. Because mystery speaks of the unknowable, the insoluble and that which transcends the limits of human reason, we are inclined to regard it glibly as a relic of an unenlightened age. We forget that we are a mystery unto ourselves and that our minds are but tiny grains of sand, whereas the reality of God is as great as the ocean. No matter what we say about God, he is so much more, for he is awe-inspiring, the deepest mystery of our life beyond the reach of time. In contemplating God we are out of our depth and can only fumble in the dark in search of glimmers of light. God is not one whom we have come to know as a result of our clever reasoning. We could not even have got a glimpse into the heart of God had he not revealed and disclosed himself to us first.

Trinity Sunday celebrates the unbounded mystery of God who as Creator, Saviour and Sanctifier is a centre of love, which overflows and touches the whole of creation. The three persons in the Trinity are so enveloped in each other that they are perfectly one. Love begins in the Father who created us and cares so deeply about us that he sent his only Son into the world as a brother who died for our sakes and is poured out into our hearts by the Holy Spirit who sanctifies us. Their closeness is a model for the relationships we must have as Christians for we are enveloped in that love and challenged to give it expression in our community. This means relating to each other in love, unity and harmony. Whenever we show love through our actions to someone close in our family or in our neighbourhood, this is just a small reflection of the love that the Holy Trinity has for us. As we go about our everyday activities we sense something of that mystery of love working for us, affecting the core of our lives and strengthening us in our weakness.

The mystery of the Trinity tells us something remarkable about who we are and how we ought to live. There is only one God and we are made in his image and likeness. It might help us to remember that on the day of our baptism, as members of this distinguished family we were sent out on a mission in the name of the Father, Son and Holy Spirit, to announce that God so loved the world that he sent us his only Son so that through him the world might be saved. This morning, as we immerse ourselves in the mystery and the wonder of God in three persons whom we worship and adore, our hope is that we shall become like him and share in his glory. In the meantime we look forward to the day when we shall see you, our God, as you are.

Prayer of the Faithful

Celebrant: As a community united in faith, hope and charity, we turn to the Father and place before him out needs and cares.

1. We pray that Our Holy Father, bishops and priests may proclaim the one true God to the world by being faithful to the will of the Father, obedient to the teachings of Jesus Christ and sensitive to the promptings of the Holy Spirit.
    Lord, hear us.

2. That the unifying love of Father, Son and Holy Spirit may draw together in mutual harmony the people of our neighbourhoods.
    Lord, hear us.

3. As many young people prepare for examinations, we pray that the Holy Spirit will inspire them, ease their anxiety and grant them success.
    Lord, hear us.

4. We pray for the sick, the old and those living on the fringe of life. May they experience the compassion of Jesus through those who care for them.
    Lord, hear us.

5. We pray that those who have died may share fully in the heavenly banquet with the perpetual light of God always shining on them.
    Lord, hear us.

Heavenly Father, we acknowledge you as one God in three persons. Hear our petitions so that the life of the Trinity may be reflected in us. We ask this through Christ, our Lord. Amen.

The Feast of the Body and Blood of Christ

First Reading: Deuteronomy 8:2-3. 14-16
Second Reading: 1 Corinthians 10:16-17; Gospel: John 6:51-58

One day at Capernaum when Jesus was talking to his disciples he made the claim, 'He who eats my flesh and drinks my blood lives in me and I live in him.' He was, in a remote way, preparing them for the mystery of the Eucharist. Some felt uncomfortable with the claim and parted company with him. The disciples who remained did not fully understand what he meant but they trusted that he spoke the truth. It was not until the end of the meal on Holy Thursday evening when Jesus took bread and wine and declared that he was the living bread come down from heaven, that they got a glimpse of what he meant that day. The words Jesus said over the bread and wine changed what was ordinary food and drink into his whole person. Ever since, his followers have been breaking and sharing bread in his memory as their central act of Christian worship.

Today the universal church celebrates Christ's amazing and abiding presence in the Eucharist being linked with food and drink, the sustenance of human life. Only a loving God could have given us such an unimaginable gift. This is a splendid occasion to immerse ourselves in mystery, and reflect on God's most striking gift of himself to us, under the appearance of bread and wine. Taking time out to marvel at the wonder of the touchingly human thing he did on that Thursday night, when he shared a meal with his close friends, prevents us from taking for granted so precious a gift as the Body of Christ. On this the feast of Corpus Christi we are repeating the Last Supper celebration but we are doing so in a joyful manner which was not at all possible during Holy Week, with the shadow of the cross looming large.

The feast of Corpus Christi reminds us that at each Mass we are guests of the Lord and his invitation to take and eat is as strong today as it was two thousand years ago. Nowhere is the Lord so completely present among his followers as he is at the breaking of bread. The Eucharist is a meal involving real food and real drink where we discover our greatest heritage as Christians. It is not a memory of things past but is a making present to each generation the great act of salvation. We must always remember that Christ instituted the Eucharist as food. Just as bread nourishes the life of the body, the Eucharist nourishes the life of the spirit and is food for our journeying through the wilderness as we make our way towards eternal life. Christ in his role of friendship comes to us as forgiveness for past wrong doings, as support for present trials and as a pledge of future glory.

Eucharist on Sunday without shared life on Monday is suspect because it indicates that the face and heart of God are not getting an opportunity to emerge from our lives. The Eucharist reminds us of the personal and social relationships that bind us one to another. Communion involves an expression of togetherness in community and is an invitation to bring the compassionate love of Christ to our neighbours and friends. We are being less than the Body of Christ if we recognise Christ at the altar under the appearance of bread and wine while ignoring his presence in our brothers and sisters. There is no one who does not experience upsets every day caused either by personal carelessness or by the annoyance of neighbours. Our whole lives are made up of little incidents of this kind, producing a host of feelings of dislike, envy and fear, which trouble the peace of our minds. Someone close passes an incautious remark, we are irritated so we retaliate and break a friendship. The Eucharist affords us an opportunity to offer all these petty annoyances to God, asking his forgiveness for what we have done wrong and permitting us to set out once more on the pathway of reconciliation. The extent to which we draw spiritual sustenance from the breaking of bread in the Eucharist depends on our openness to caring, sharing and having respect for the disadvantaged in our midst. If the Eucharist is to mean anything to us we have to put into practise what we are celebrating in the ups and downs of life. It will involve walking on the road travelled by Christ, which was one of loving service. The Feast of Corpus Christi speaks to us of the love from which all love flows.

Prayer of the Faithful

Celebrant: Celebrating the feast of Christ's own Body and Blood, we stand with confidence in the presence of God the Father and make our petitions to him.

1. We pray that the church throughout the world may grow in the appreciation of the Eucharist as the Bread of Life by celebrating the sacrifice of the Mass with greater meaning and devotion.
   Lord, hear us.

2. That, fed on the Body and Blood of the Lord, all the people in this congregation may play their part in promoting love, justice and peace within the community.
   Lord, hear us.

3. Let us pray to the Lord to bless all children who at this time are making their first communion.
   Lord, hear us.

4. We pray for the lonely who hunger for companionship and the sick who hunger for health that the Lord may grant them the spiritual comfort of his healing presence in the Eucharist.
   Lord, hear us.

5. For those who have died, that they may reap the rewards of their faithfulness by sharing in eternal peace.
   Lord, hear us.

Heavenly Father, on this day when we celebrate the feast of your Son's permanent presence amongst us, we pray for a deeper appreciation of our need of his nourishment. We ask this through Christ, our Lord. Amen.

Second Sunday in Ordinary Time
First Reading: Isaiah 49:3, 5-6;
Second Reading: 1 Corinthians 1:1-3; Gospel: John 1:29-34

We are introduced to Isaiah, Paul and John the Baptist, three people who were chosen by God for specific purposes in life. Isaiah's vocation was to be a leader of the Israelites in exile who would give them encouragement and new heart at a time when their resolve appeared weak and their morale was low. He was to be a light to the nations proclaiming God's salvation to the ends of the earth. Paul was favoured as an apostle and as a man of mission he extended God's invitation to the people of Corinth to embark on a life of holiness, which was their calling. John the Baptist was the first witness to Christ. The gospel setting is the river Jordan where John was preparing a group of Israelites for the coming of the Messiah. His guidance was crystal clear and everyone sensed from the stern tone of his preaching, that something significant was about to happen. As John stood on the bank he looked up and on seeing Jesus coming towards him exclaimed, 'Behold the Lamb of God who takes away the sins of the world.' It was not until that very moment, when the Spirit descended on Jesus in the form of a dove, that John became aware of his cousin as the long awaited Messiah. The pointing out of Jesus as the Lamb of God was a grace-filled occasion. Christ's arrival was John's finest hour for his mission of stage-managing the greatest event of all time was completed. All that remained for him to do was to bow out and slip gracefully into the background. 'He must increase, and I must decrease.'

Through their individual spiritual experiences Isaiah, Paul and John the Baptist, have different ways of expressing God's calling and the manner in which we, as followers are invited to respond. Sanctity is the duty of every Christian and not the exceptional characteristic of a few. Every individual person has a vocation and a purpose in life but whether or not we achieve that goal is in our own hands and up to ourselves. Life's journey is different for everyone. Each path has its own joys and particular crisis, its own satisfaction and seemingly intractable problems. If we are to become what God wants us to be, our personal choices are the most significant factors in the movement toward that end. These daily choices taken so frequently as we journey, move us ever closer or further away from God's plan. It is the everyday insignificant happenings that establish our lifestyle and reveal our priorities as a person. Jesus' message is that heaven must begin here and now in the familiar experiences of this life. The extent to which we manage to transform our lives in accordance with his ways will show the depth of the spirituality we have achieved. Day by day we have to chip away at our selfishness in order to make room for Christ's unselfish love. We become what God wants us to be as we learn to practise little acts of kindness and discover ways of sharing love while doing the ordinary chores of daily life. Because God works through ordinary agents like us, our actions and good example speak louder than words. There is a need to show a purpose in human living and to point the way for people towards true happiness.

This gospel reminds us of the crucial role we play in leading others to Christ. If God is in our hearts, he goes wherever we go. We are called to bring a deep commitment to Christian ideals to a society of shifting values. For the truth of God to be accessible to others, the Christian life must not be restricted to church worship but must spread out into our neighbourhood and workplace. The Christian calling invites each generation to hand on the faith to the next. There is the need to take stock, to look at where we are going and what are we about, otherwise we run the danger of just drifting along in an aimless fashion. True sanctity involves accepting ourselves as we are and using our talents creatively to build up the kingdom of God. As Christ becomes the centrepiece of our life we sense the importance of being in touch with him through prayer and an honest admission of our failures so as to become his instruments of salvation. Following Christ is not easy. There is no room for a half-hearted effort. It demands nothing less than absolute loyalty and a complete commitment. 'Here I am Lord, I come to do your will.'

Prayer of the Faithful

Celebrant: Gathered here as a community that seeks to bear witness to the coming of the Lamb of God, we place our needs before God the Father.

1. For the church, may it be persistent in its mission to bring the light of faith to all nations.
   Lord, hear us.

2. We pray for those who are burdened with guilt from the past. May Christ, who takes away the sin of the world, grant them peace.
   Lord, hear us.

3. We pray for parents that they may realise their special mission of discipleship in handing on the faith to their children.
   Lord, hear us.

4. That all those who are sick and suffering may come to know that God the Father cares for them and that they are precious in his eyes.
   Lord, hear us.

5. We pray for the dead who have followed Jesus through the gateway of death. May they enjoy God's presence forever in heaven.
   Lord, hear us.

Lord, make us always thankful for the message of love, which came to us through your Son Jesus Christ. Let it become the source of living power in our lives, through Christ, our Lord. Amen.

Third Sunday in Ordinary Time
First Reading: Isaiah 8:23-9:3;
Second reading: 1 Corinthians: 10-13, 17; Gospel: Matthew 4:12-23

At about the age of thirty Jesus left the hillside village of
Nazareth, where he had grown up, and settled down in
Capernaum by the lakeside, where a fisherman named Peter
had his home. He was never again to handle a hammer or ply his
trade as a carpenter. Thereafter his principal occupation would
be preaching, teaching, healing, calling people to repentance
and training others to follow in his footsteps. Up and down
Galilee in synagogues, on hillsides, by the lakeshore, wherever
he found a group to listen, Jesus moved among people healing
the sick, comforting the distressed and tirelessly proclaiming the
good news. In a world torn apart at every level by strife, greed
and pride his words brought hope and were an urgent message
directed towards conversion and salvation. People were drawn
by his presence, travelled for miles to hear his message, and sat
entranced for hours as he explained the deepest mysteries of
heaven in the simplest imagery of household, field and lake. He
was a healer who could place his hand on a fevered forehead
and in an instant bring refreshing coolness. His enthusiasm for
preaching and his insistence on repentance never faded. Small
wonder that sinners were among his most fervent fans. They
desperately wanted what he promised – a fresh start and a new
beginning. Above all he restored damaged souls, offered forgiveness and comfort to sinners, and dispelled their doubt and
despair.

The launching of Jesus into his public ministry involved the
forming of a community that would not only keep his teachings
intact but would continue the work he had begun, by being his
living presence among humankind. His mission was to be accomplished through a group who believed, accepted and experienced salvation through him. It has often been said that God
moves in mysterious ways and uses the weak to confront the
strong. When he set about selecting his disciples he looked for
them among run of the mill people who lived ordinary, everyday lives. Peter, Andrew, James and John were chosen, with no
special training or without any merit on their part, to be core

members of that community. Up to that moment the world of boats, nets and fish was their place of belonging. It provided a decent living and they never dreamed of a different lifestyle. Now their mission was to bring the knowledge and love of Christ to the whole world. Their response was immediate and a complete act of willing co-operation. As a group they had little to recommend them apart from their hearts being in the right place, and having an inner awareness of the goodness of Jesus and a desire to remain in his company. They did not know what they were letting themselves in for but when Jesus called they were ready to take risks and became a God-driven force that would change the world.

Like the apostles we too have a great task on our hands. We are called to be servants of God, bearers of the good news and builders of his kingdom of peace and joy. If the word of God is to reach everyone then all who hear it must make it known. There is simply no one who is not called to be a disciple. Christ wants us all to be part of his saving mission and yet there are so many good hearted people unaware of the part they can play as messengers of the good news. We don't have to go looking in far off places to carry out God's will. The opportunity to respond to it is most likely to be present in our nearest and dearest and shows up more often that we think. A mother teaching her child to pray is a messenger of the gospel, fulfilling the responsibility of her baptismal calling. If we live the life of Christ in our homes our words will surely mirror something of the face of God and bring compassion and comfort to the sick. In a world of darkness, where people are living lives of quiet desperation, fearful of the future and searching to make sense of it all, our presence can brighten up the road ahead with reassurance and peace. We are reminded that as members of the Body of Christ we have a role to play and a job to do. If we take our personal call seriously and have the courage to respond, then the kingdom of God will surely be in our midst.

Prayer of the Faithful

Celebrant: We offer our prayers and petitions to God our Father as a pilgrim people seeking to love him more fully and serve him more completely.

1. We pray that the spiritual leaders in the church may challenge the faithful to live more fully in the ways of Christ.
   Lord, hear us.

2. We pray for the young people of our community. May they be generous in their response to God's call and offer themselves to his service in the priesthood and religious life.
   Lord, hear us.

3. Let us pray that, like the people who walked in darkness in Galilee, we, in our time, will experience the light of Christ.
   Lord, hear us.

4. May we bring the joy of Christ's friendship to the bereaved, the separated and those who do not experience the love of family and friends.
   Lord, hear us.

5. We commend to God's loving care our relatives and friends who have gone before us, marked with the sign of the cross.
   Lord, hear us.

Almighty God, grant that we, your faithful people, may never cease in the work of establishing your kingdom on earth and so come to the joys of your eternal homeland. We make our prayer through Christ, our Lord. Amen.

Fourth Sunday in Ordinary Time
First Reading: Zephaniah 2:3, 3:12-13
Second Reading: 1 Corinthians 1:26-31; Gospel: Matthew 5:1-12

There can be few more challenging passages in the scriptures to measure our attitudes and actions against than the Beatitudes. In vivid and poetic language Matthew sets before us the values that will transform our lives into the likeness of Christ. However, they are such a familiar part of our religious heritage that we can easily miss their meaning. There is every chance that we will listen to the Beatitudes and leave them aside without confronting ourselves as to their relevance, because we don't want to be bothered, as they seem impossible. To attain the standards they propose would mean having to walk the life Jesus set before us. Our instinct is to reject something that cuts across the human grain of selfishness within us and is so contrary to the way society has conditioned the culture of our age. We regard them as an ideal and heroic formula for life and discard them because we have our feet firmly on the ground and are not the stuff heroes or idealists are made of. It is not in our nature to take such risks. In the cut and thrust of the world, the ideals proposed in the Beatitudes contradict our common-sense approach to things and have little place in the life of the modern day disciple.

Meanwhile we are content to search for earthly pleasures, snatching at every possible comfort in a feverish effort to find the security and happiness we yearn for. We barely notice that the worldly values we strive after cannot bring us contentment. Happiness has nothing to do with wealth or levels of education and is something larger and more lasting than cheap and passing thrills. While we don't have to be poor to be happy, it still remains a fact of experience that property, power, high position, and prestige do not bring inner peace. It is not easy to find happiness in ourselves but it is impossible to find it elsewhere. Deep within the human heart there is a restlessness amidst all the escapism on offer, which is never satisfied. The pursuit of happiness is a search and a desire for something that this earth cannot give. If we want happiness – and who doesn't – the world is the wrong place to go looking for it. All this shows how far we have got to go in letting our lives be remade and refashioned according to this gospel, which states that Christ alone can bring us happiness. It calls us to the mystery of the cross as it speaks about the real world and does not deny hardship, struggle or pain. We are told that the most valuable things in life have to be purchased with sacrifice. What is more, God does not want success from us but only our faithfulness.

Each of the Beatitudes deals with a different aspect of human life. Qualities like meekness, gentleness, and being merciful may at first sight indicate weakness but reflection will bear out that they demand strength of character and sturdy determination. To make peace and offer reconciliation requires firmness of character when the easier option is to lose one's temper, cause a row and exact revenge. If we are courageous enough to stand our ground and uphold a friend's reputation that is being torn to shreds, then we know what hungering and thirsting for justice is all about. While meekness and gentleness might not help us climb the ladder of success in the workplace, we witness the strength of the gentle and the patience of the meek in compassionate carers who devote endless hours to looking after the elderly and the sick at home and in hospital. We find God wherever people are treated with courtesy, respect and kindness. Grieving for a loved one may be painful but in the process our loss is acknowledged and we are healed. Looking back, how often have we found that the events that have shaped our lives, given us inner strength and made us the people we are, were not the triumphant stories of success but the times of failure, disappointment and sorrow. They were grace-filled moments of brokenness when God touched us, filled us with his Spirit, made us more mature persons with compassion and understanding and better able to appreciate other people's plights. The Beatitudes are the great jewel of the gospel which heaps blessings on those who put them into practice in daily life. They are a call to live the universal love, total forgiveness and unselfish generosity of God as expressed in the words and actions of Jesus Christ.

Prayer of the Faithful

Celebrant: In the poverty and emptiness of our hearts, we turn now to God our Father and place before him our petitions.

1. That bishops and priests may have the courage to preach and teach the message of the gospels.
   Lord, hear us.

2. Let us pray for those who are persecuted in the cause of right. May they remain steadfast and true to the teachings of God's kingdom.
   Lord, hear us.

3. That the disadvantaged in our community, may find a place of dignity and contentment among us.
   Lord, hear us.

4. Lord, help us in the coming week to give comfort to a neighbour, food to the hungry and encouragement to the depressed.
   Lord, hear us.

5. We pray that our beloved dead, who are freed from the anxieties of life, may enjoy everlasting peace in heaven.
   Lord, hear us.

Heavenly Father, hear our prayers that we humbly place before you. Help us always to be poor in spirit, trusting completely in you, so that we may be filled with your unending love. We ask this through Christ, our Lord. Amen.

Fifth Sunday in Ordinary Time
First reading: Isaiah 58:7-12; Second Reading: 1 Corinthians 2:1-5
Gospel: Matthew 5:13-16

The amount of confusion and helplessness a power failure can cause within a domestic set up is truly amazing. I happened to be visiting a family recently when a complete black out occurred. The first thing everyone tried to do was to look for a light. Ordinary everyday activities within the home, like watching TV, listening to music, playing computer games and reading a book suddenly ground to a standstill and family members had to resort to engaging one another in meaningful conversation.

Light is probably one of the most vital things in our experience. It is something we take for granted and do not notice until suddenly we are without it. Living as town dwellers we don't often get the opportunity to experience total darkness, to look heavenwards and appreciate the stars. The creation story in the Bible tells how darkness covered the face of the earth until God spoke and said, 'Let there be light.' Ever since, light and darkness have been powerful symbols representing good and evil as well as the presence and the absence of God.

At the beginning of St John's gospel Jesus is referred to as the true light come into the world to enlighten all men. Coming from darkness into the light expresses that dramatic change that is expected in our Christian life in the way we speak to and treat other people, carry out our work, pay our bills and avoid all types of shady behaviour. We are called to walk in the light of Christ, bringing forth fruits of goodness, justice and truth. Jesus wants the whole world to be transformed by the good example of those people who live by his gospel. Whatever our state in life – married, single, working or unemployed – our Christianity should be clearly evident in every part of our lives. Being a follower of Christ is not about being in the shadows or hiding in the wings. People who have strayed into darkness need to rediscover the lost radiance of their Christian faith. We must not underestimate our witness because our good works will not pass unnoticed but will make a difference by encouraging others to do likewise and shed Christ's light into the world. As discipleship can never be a merely private affair people will see the light of God in and through us according to the way we behave. There should be a sheer sparkle about our Christian lives for we were born to make manifest the glory of God that is within us and every step of our pilgrim journey is meant to bring us closer to the fullness of that light.

It is a fair challenge that Jesus issues when he tells us to move out of our own little worlds and enter the worry of another person's fears, the anxiety of a friend's uncertainty and the sadness of a neighbour's mourning. When we can truly say to one another that your pain is my pain, your hope is my hope and your sorrow is my sadness, then we are sharing the burdens of each other's lives. It is then that we are truly being Christian.

'Salt of the earth' is a proverbial phrase like 'as good as gold' and is one of the highest compliments of our language. Long before the kitchen freezer became an essential item in the home, salt was the great preservative that fended off all sources of decay and guaranteed the nourishing goodness of food over a lengthy period of time. In the ancient world salt was very highly valued and was the commonest of all preservatives. The Romans of old had a saying 'nothing is more precious than sun and salt' and often included salt among their offerings to the gods. When Jesus Christ called his followers the salt of the earth he was indicating how highly he prized them and the greatness they were capable of achieving. As salt adds flavour to food, Christians are to make a difference to the lives of others in their particular environment by their very presence. The salt of truth alone can protect mind and heart and save us from all shades of darkness and despair that corrupt and kill. In an age when many are unable to distinguish right from wrong, good from evil, truth from falsehood each of us is challenged to be both salt and light and as visible in genuine goodness as a city set upon a hilltop. We are called to witness to the world that we are God's people reflecting the radiance of his glory.

Prayer of the Faithful

Celebrant: Having listened to the gospel calling us to be 'the salt of the earth and the light of the world', we turn to God the Father and pray that, by our actions, we may always be a beacon of light shining in the darkness.

1. For our Holy Father, bishops and priests, that they may lead God's people with patience and perseverance.
   Lord, hear us.

2. We pray that this community will make every effort to be the salt of the earth and light of the world, by sharing its material goods with the poor and the needy.
   Lord, hear us.

3. We pray that all people who have strayed into the darkness of despair will rediscover the radiance of their Christian faith.
   Lord, hear us.

4. That Christ may enlighten all who seek the truth as they journey on their pilgrim way.
   Lord, hear us.

5. For those saddened by the death of a loved one: that the words of Christ may bring them peace and consolation in the difficult days ahead.
   Lord, hear us.

Heavenly Father, may the love we share and the service we show to others be a reflection of your glory shining in and through us. We ask that you hear and answer our prayers through Christ, our Lord. Amen.

Sixth Sunday in Ordinary Time
First Reading: Ecclesiasticus 15:15-20;
Second Reading: 1 Corinthians 2:6-10; Gospel: Matthew 5:17-37

The message of Jesus never ceases to amaze us. His association with sinners made him suspect in the eyes of fellow Israelites. Even more damaging was his attitude to religious Law when he healed on the Sabbath and made light of the ceremonial washing of hands before meals, both of which drew the ire of the scribes and Pharisees who observed them scrupulously. For most Jews the law was the ultimate revelation of God and a secure guide to good conduct. Small wonder then, that some of his listeners must have been surprised when he declared that he came, not to abolish the Law and the Prophets, but to complete them. Moreover, to be saved they would need to be more virtuous than the scribes and Pharisees, too many of whom were paying no more than lip service to the commandments. Jesus saw his role as fulfilling the law and bringing it to perfection by broadening the scope of the commandments and forcing us to look beyond our actions to our attitudes. He was pointing out that it is not just deeds that fall under God's judgement but motives also and that outward actions should flow from proper motives, convictions and dispositions. Getting by within the letter of the law is not what Jesus had in mind. Far from being whittled down he presents the commandments in a more challenging fashion. Their demands are even sharpened to the point of the near impossible as Jesus calls for a virtue that has deep roots in the human heart, stating that if our intentions are good and pure, then the actions coming from our hearts will flow from love. He is telling us that if we keep opening ourselves to the Spirit of God's love, then our every action will reflect something of the life-giving quality of Christ himself. In other words, what we say and do must express what is in our hearts. So whatever about knowing the name and number of the Ten Commandments, it is more important to appreciate the value that lies behind each. Christ wants us to purify our intentions and move away from external appearances and observances. The real standard is whether or not our motives are sincere. We can fool others with a good and charitable act but not God or our conscience.

As churchgoers we are being challenged to look carefully at our lives – not merely at what we do, but at the thoughts and motivation behind our behaviour towards others. Are we merely fulfilling the law of external observance because of a failure to mend a difference with a neighbour? If reconciliation is a sacred duty and we cannot reach out our hand in friendship to someone in our community with whom we are quarrelling, how can we reach out our hand to receive Christ in the Eucharist? Our relationships are so important with ourselves, others and with God. All these relationships spring from our attitudes of heart and mind. Take marriage for instance. The avoidance of adultery is not the key to a good marriage. Adultery is born in the heart and only someone looking merely to the letter of the law would be satisfied with a marriage in which neither party committed adultery. There must be such loving and constant trust between the spouses that neither looks at someone else with thoughts and desires of lust in their heart.

As for murder, it is not enough for the Christian to observe the ruling not to kill or do violence to one's neighbour. Murder is more than just the taking of a man's life. It is the ultimate outgrowth of anger, hatred and wicked feelings with roots in bigotry and bitterness, which erupt in a moment of uncontrollable violence. If murder is reprehensible, so are its sources. Anyone who nurses grudges, harbours resentment and seeks revenge can easily drift into anger and hatred to the point of murder. The follower of Jesus may not think, plan or say any evil against another human being. We need to take from our hearts the plotting and the planning of those deeds which is as evil as pulling the trigger. There is more to this gospel than meets the eye. The search for personal meaning and fulfilment continues in life. When we look within ourselves we realise the long way we have to go on the road to Christian maturity. Keeping up appearances will never do, as there is no room in Christianity for doing the bare minimum.

Prayer of the Faithful

Celebrant: Inspired by the words, 'Ask and you shall receive' we turn with confidence to God our Father as we make our requests.

1. We pray that God may sustain bishops, priests and religious in their work of spreading his kingdom here on earth.
   Lord, hear us.

2. That all parents, teachers and those responsible for education may guide our young people to the way of Christ with patience, understanding and love.
   Lord, hear us.

3. During this week, we ask for the generosity to reach out the hand of friendship to those with whom we have had a difference of opinion.
   Lord, hear us.

4. For the sick, the housebound and the depressed that, by uniting their sufferings with Christ, they may find an inner peace and contentment.
   Lord, hear us.

5. That the faithful departed, who carried their cross in this life, may reap the reward of eternal life.
   Lord, hear us.

Almighty Father, hear our prayers, spoken and unspoken. May we resolve to serve you more faithfully. We ask this through Christ, our Lord. Amen.

Seventh Sunday in Ordinary Time
First Reading: Leviticus 19:1-2, 17-18
Second Reading: 1 Corinthians 3:16-32; Gospel: Matthew 5:38-48

I don't know what you think about this gospel, but it would be hard to find another passage in scripture which is so much at odds with our normal way of behaving. Loving our friends is easy enough, but when Jesus speaks about turning the other cheek and embracing the very people who have injured us, hurt us, and have shown no appreciation for our kindness, this is an extravagance which goes beyond our human way of dealing with things, and sets up an ideal too difficult to achieve. Turning the other cheek is a risky business and it can be interpreted as cowardice, a failure to stand up to a bully and consequently an invitation to pile on more of the same abuse. It is no wonder that people regard it as their natural right to return evil for evil. The urge to seek revenge, to hit back and level the score is instinctive and almost second nature. I am sure most of us find this gospel speaking to us very directly, for we all have enemies, from the meddlesome neighbour, to the business rival, to the family feud over a will, to the classmate we cannot stand and to the relationship that is in tatters. They are very much to the forefront of our mind for the reluctance to forgive and the rush to judgement is alive and well in every age. We may be disappointed that Jesus is asking us to take that additional step and walk that extra mile in loving those who deliberately exclude us from their social circles, who talk behind our backs, make us feel inferior and treat us with contempt. Since we seem to be engaged in a rearguard action, well might we ask what is the point of demanding perfection in an age of chronic imperfection especially when we don't see any results from our efforts? God is calling us in countless ways to change and go beyond what appears reasonable. He wants us to develop strength of character in order to forgive and refrain from hitting back and levelling the score. There is ample evidence around us of the devastating effects of life lived according to the rule of an eye for an eye. We have only got to think of the energy we waste holding on to past hurts, trying to settle old scores, or even worse, handing down grudges from one generation to the next. Hatred does not add to our stature but tears us apart, because once we retaliate and start hating our enemies we give them power over us, which can turn our days and nights into a hellish turmoil. However, when we manage to let go of the hatred within our hearts and become loving people we do things differently. We develop a kind tongue, a soft touch which enables us to overlook faults, refuse to pass judgement and discover the good qualities in people.

This is nothing less than a gospel call to holiness, 'To be perfect as our heavenly Father is perfect.' Holiness seems far removed from our everyday lives. We tend to look upon it as an other-worldly quality, which is far beyond our reach and the distinguishing mark of the monk, the religious and the saint. As average Christians who are doing our best to make spiritual ends meet we limit our notion of holiness to daily prayers and attendance at Sunday Mass. We fail to identify holiness as something which is within our reach and that can be lived and experienced in ordinary everyday life. Holiness is about putting God at the centre of our lives and being aware of his heart beat in the people around us. We become holy by doing the simple things like a mother taking care of her children and turning her house into a home. People who go to work each day, students who devote time to their studies and those caring for the sick and elderly achieve a high degree of holiness in the circumstance of their everyday life. Holiness is not so much in what we do, as the love with which we do it. Day by day we have got to chip away at our selfishness to make way for loving as Christ loves. Like a sculptor who little by little chisels away at a huge chunk of stone until the image grows more and more into the beautiful creation he has in mind, so it is with us. Little by little as we develop a Christ-like love, we gradually become what God wants us to be. In that way God turns from being a Sunday acquaintance into a weekday friend.

Prayer of the Faithful

Celebrant: Conscious that Jesus aske us to be perfect as our heavenly Father is perfect, we place our prayers before God the Father and ask for his help.

1. That the leaders of the church may reflect God's holiness in the world by giving witness in the ways of love, pardon and forgiveness.
   Lord, hear us.

2. That those who are angry and bitter with their neighbours may realise that giving way to feelings of resentment and hatred also separates them from God.
   Lord, hear us.

3. For those who search for truth that they may embrace the mystery of God in the people they come in contact with daily.
   Lord, hear us.

4. May God's love bring hope and comfort to those living in the grip of worry and despair.
   Lord, hear us.

5. May the faithful departed receive the generous rewards of their labours in their heavenly home.
   Lord, hear us.

Almighty Father, you know our weaknesses. Rid our hearts of all bitterness and bless our efforts to love all people. We make our prayer through Christ, our Lord. Amen.

Eighth Sunday in Ordinary Time
First reading: Isaiah 49:14-15; Second Reading: 1 Corinthians 4:1-5
Gospel: Matthew 6:24-34

We get a rare glimpse into the life and times of Jesus as we listen to his poetic description of the Heavenly Father's loving care for the birds of the air and flowers in the fields. It reveals his appreciation of the creation that was all around him. He had time to observe the rise and fall of the seasons and this makes us wonder what it would be like to live in a less hurried age. Most of us live in a muddle, full of uncertainties and are totally bewildered about what is happening all around us while we try to cope as best we can in a period of rapid change and instant satisfaction of desires. Ours is an age of anxiety marked by disquiet and misgiving. We are all concerned about the future of our jobs, about the health of our families and what is going to happen to our children. The world beyond our front door is a threatening place.

We've never had it so good. In an era of unprecedented wealth, we have become preoccupied with amassing material possessions, and defining ourselves more by what we have than by who we are. Sadly we have discovered that the route to happiness turns out to be elusive. We go looking for happiness in the wrong places. Taking the waiting out of wanting hasn't helped. There is little doubt that something has gone wrong. We are faced with the paradox of why if things appear to be so good, are they so bad? The fact is that we have gone astray and in achieving our selfish goal we have neglected the spiritual, have kept God out of the picture and as a result have lost our moral and spiritual bearings.

The gospel is bringing home to us the message that there is more to life than the food we eat, the designer clothes we wear or the possessions we hoard. It points out that we are in constant danger of becoming immersed in the affairs of this world and of allowing them to enslave us. God alone can satisfy. He is our rock, our stronghold and our fortress and in him alone do we find rest. There is an empty space within the human heart, and that can only be filled by God. However, we will not realise this unless we seek opportunities to escape from the frantic web of everyday living in order to stand back and see what is of greater or lesser importance. Only then can we discover that God is close to us all day long and has built into us an intimacy with him that is quite astonishing. His love, which is beaming down on us, is without limits and is stronger than a mother's love for her child. He cares for the world with a care that never ceases. Time out to observe a sunset, to view an ocean or gaze up at a starry sky will bring home how we are a tiny but meaningful speck of his creation. Although we may seem insignificant, we are nevertheless, a fragment of God's presence in the world, most precious in his eyes, and assured of his everlasting love.

A message that comes across loud and clear is that worry must not cloud out our vision of the meaning of life. Our spirit must always be free to reach out to God and not become bogged down by the pursuit of material needs. Each day is to be lived as it comes, each task to be carried out as it appears. God will provide. This does not mean that we should sit back and do nothing or that reasonable concern about providing for our daily needs is not necessary. Jesus is not advocating a reckless and thoughtless attitude to life. The quality of our effort is most important. He is telling us to get our priorities right because our longing for a security that endures cannot be satisfied by the things that do not endure. The danger of becoming engrossed in acquiring the luxuries of life is that we can lose sight of the value of life itself. We have a way of allowing material things to become our master, letting them blind us to the grace of God and the needs of others. The basic question is whether God comes first and is the undisputed master of our lives? Serving God offers us a life where we are secure in his love and free from unnecessary worry.

Prayer of the Faithful

Celebrant: Placing aside our worries and anxieties, we bring our innermost needs before God the Father who cares for the whole of creation and in whom we live and move and have our being.

1. We pray that our Holy Father and all bishops, priests and religious may always serve the church with integrity and love.
   Lord, hear us.

2. For all who hold positions of responsibility, that they may become aware of the needs of those who are unable to care for themselves.
   Lord, hear us.

3. May all who are called to follow Christ live at peace with one another in an atmosphere of mutual respect and trust.
   Lord, hear us.

4. For the sick, the weary and those without hope, that God may give them the strength to face the future.
   Lord, hear us.

5. We pray for the dead who have touched our lives in so many ways and whose faith is known to God alone. May they rejoice with Jesus forever in his heavenly kingdom.
   Lord, hear us.

Heavenly Father, your love touches our lives at every single moment. May we always appreciate the blessings you shower upon us. We make our prayer through Christ, the Lord. Amen.

Ninth Sunday in Ordinary Time
First Reading: Deuteronomy 11:18, 26-28;
Second Reading: Romans 3:21-25, 28; Gospel: Matthew 7:21-27

Nowadays it is very easy to live a shallow existence, to go along with the flow and adopt the current fashions. Among other things it means that we don't have to do any serious thinking for ourselves and we will not cause any ripples of controversy by holding views that are different from our friends. All of this is a far cry from the schooling Jesus has just finished giving his disciples in what is commonly known as the Sermon on the Mount. In it, Christ is making a call for the disciples to examine the way they live and a plea for his words to be taken seriously. Jesus is inviting them to base their lives entirely on his message which is an expression of the will of God the Father. They are to love their enemies, pray for their persecutors and harbour no thoughts of revenge for injuries received. It is a call to live in human terms the universal love, total forgiveness and unselfish generosity as expressed in the life and actions of Jesus. The deep compassion that he showed towards the poor, the blind and the handicapped is something they will have to imitate in their own lives. Their task is to put his words and actions into practice before an unbelieving world. At the end of time the Almighty God will not judge them on the knowledge they have acquired, the fame they have won or the wealth they have amassed. He will be more interested in the help they have given to the marginalised and in the ways they were loving and generous. A lot will depend on the performance or neglect of these acts of mercy.

It is decision time for the disciples; they have a choice to make. Talking has to give way to action and theory needs to be put into practice. Service has to be grounded in solid commitment. We are in a similar situation. If we take the Lord's words into our hearts and souls, make them our own and live by them, we are blessed with having a rock-like foundation which will withstand every storm that life is liable to throw at us. However, to continually think, talk and act in a Godly manner is most challenging. The problem arises because the ways of the world are completely different from the values of the gospel. While we agree that it is most laudable to banish hatred from our heart so as to live in perfect harmony within the community, the problem arises with the personal hostility that exists within our own family. This running sore has long since destroyed all lines of communication but none of us has the humility to pocket our pride and start speaking to one another again. We may be pilgrims on the road of life in need of the forgiveness of God but we have a blind spot when it comes to seeking forgiveness from our brother. We have no quarrel with insisting on an honest day's pay for an honest day's work but what about the short cuts we take and the times we ring in sick unnecessarily?

Christ was showing a deep understanding of human nature when he said not everyone who says, 'Lord, Lord,' will enter the kingdom of heaven. He was in no way fooled by appearances as he could see into the depth of the human heart. Sincerity and openness appealed to him. In contrast, our capacity for self-deception is truly astounding; each of us likes to think that we are better than we are. All of us are in constant danger of pretending to be religious and pious but not living up to our ideals. Very few of us can say that our deeds always match our words. All too often we make a vague intention to act out Christ's words but end up doing nothing. Calling ourselves Christians is of no avail if we do not in fact act as Christians. This is a cry for our faith life to be more than words that we hear with our ears and express with our lips.

There is a manner of living, which is the Father's will. Somehow the way we live out our commitment must be obvious to others. Nevertheless it has nothing to do with signs and wonders or the spectacular. The benchmark is the sheer sincerity in all that we do for others in the name of the Lord. There are so many in need whom we can help – residents in nursing homes who never get a visitor, single parents thirsting for friendship, lonely people crying out for someone to listen. If we have been neglectful of these duties, there is no better time to begin than now.

Prayer of the Faithful

Celebrant: God our Father we have listened to your word and now with confidence in your care and concern for each of us, we bring before you our needs and prayers.

1. We pray for our Holy Father and all the leaders of the church that they may continue to preach the message of God's love for all people.
   Lord, hear us.

2. For a deepening of our own faith and an awareness of your presence among the poor and the disadvantaged.
   Lord, hear us.

3. For young people growing up in an unstable and confusing world. Give meaning to their lives and help them to overcome failure.
   Lord, hear us.

4. For all who are coping with prolonged illness. May they be comforted by the love of God who holds them in his care.
   Lord, hear us.

5. Grant eternal rest and perpetual light to our beloved dead.
   Lord, hear us.

Heavenly Father, we ask that you continue to bless us as we strive to build your kingdom here on earth. We make our prayer through Christ, our Lord. Amen.

Tenth Sunday in Ordinary Time
First reading: Hosea 6:3-6; Second reading: Romans 4:18-25
Gospel: Matthew 9:9-13

Two characters, one depicting danger and the other opportunity represent the word *crisis* in the Chinese language. We may be enjoying a predictable pattern of living with everything going smoothly, when out of the blue something happens which changes our circumstances and sets us off on a different footing. A turning point like that happened when Jesus stood before a man called Matthew who worked as a customs officer collecting government taxes by the sea of Galilee and issued the challenge, 'Follow me.' A tax collector was the last person you would expect Jesus to choose as a disciple. Among the Jews they were moral reprobates, quislings in the employment of the Roman forces of occupation, without the slightest shred of patriotism. By their very profession tax collectors were outcasts among their own race, treated as the scum of the earth and to be avoided at all costs.

We cannot but wonder as to what it was in that glance of Jesus, which prompted Matthew to respond immediately. Maybe he never felt quite right about the life he was leading especially after standing at the edge of the crowd and overhearing the message Jesus was preaching. Perhaps his heart stirred within him as he heard the good news and wondered if it was too late to leave behind his old life of shame and begin anew. Deep down he felt a crying need for things spiritual and the call of Jesus appealed to his finest ideals. His decision to turn his back forever on his means of livelihood and join the ranks of a penniless preacher seems to have been one that he never regretted. As the road lengthened with the years, Matthew left us a gospel which has become one of the great sources of the good news about Jesus for all time.

The call of Matthew gives us a tiny insight into the ways of God. Discipleship is determined not so much by what we can do for God but rather by what God can do through us. He often chooses the most unlikely people to be his associates. While Jesus took the initiative, the remarkable factor in the story is that he flouted convention and broke the rules of society by the discernment he showed in picking Matthew as one of his close followers. Jesus saw beneath the tax collector's shady exterior the potential for goodness in a reject from society. It is an example of man judging by appearances but the Lord looking at the heart – of his ability to see beyond what people are, to what they can become. He is not so much interested in our past as in our future. The situation is made worse when Matthew's friends join Jesus at dinner. The Pharisees complain about the dubious company he keeps and show their disapproval of his preference for friends who are outside the circle of respectability. However, his response strips away all pretension and indicates how his presence heals broken lives. 'I am here not for the virtuous but for the sick and sinners.'

The call to discipleship is extended to everyone who is baptised and is not a special grace given only to a small group who have chosen a religious way of life. The story of Matthew prompts us to reflect on Christ's call in our own lives. We all have a role to play in the spreading of God's kingdom on earth. It is a challenge to turn our lives around, to follow Jesus and to proclaim his good news in the life situation in which we find ourselves. We are better to view this opening of ourselves to God's refreshing grace as an ongoing reality rather than as a once and for all happening. As our lives unfold from childhood, to young adult, from parenthood to old age and failing health we are invited at its many junctures to recommit ourselves with open eyes and faithful hearts to Christ who is beckoning us at every moment of our journey. It is an ongoing call from selfishness to generosity, from unbelief to faith and from darkness into his wonderful light. We show God to the world by following in the footsteps of Jesus Christ. Today discipleship is needed more than ever. Christ is approaching all kinds of Matthews at their occupations with his call. He speaks to the heart and calls us to the joy of service in his presence. Society around us is filled with people who feel lonely, abandoned and marginalised. We are called to help them in whatever way we can and a proper response has to be made. The church's role in the world is to proclaim to others the saving activity of God. There are a hundred ways of getting out of it. God has put himself entirely in our hands.

Prayer of the Faithful

Celebrant: As a community united in love and filled with concern for one another we call upon God our Father and ask for his help and guidance.

1. That the church and all its leaders may be strengthened by the Holy Spirit to follow their call in service to the Lord.
   Lord, hear us.

2. For those who have heard the special call of Jesus, 'Come follow me,' that they may remain faithful to their vocation.
   Lord, hear us.

3. For carers of the disadvantaged and the deprived, that they may be blessed as they bring hope and dignity to those whom they serve.
   Lord, hear us.

4. We pray for the sick and the aged. Help us to treat them always with respect and affection.
   Lord, hear us.

5. That our friends, who have completed their earthly journey, may share in the glory of Christ's resurrection.
   Lord, hear us.

Almighty and ever loving Father, we ask you to listen to our prayer and grant what is best for us, according to your will. We make our prayer through Christ, our Lord. Amen.

Eleventh Sunday in Ordinary Time
First Reading: Exodus 19:2-6; Second Reading: Romans 5:6-11
Gospel: Matthew 9:36-10:8

The casual observer might find little resemblance between the church of today and the ragged group of twelve wandering preachers whom Jesus sent out as his apostles 'to the lost sheep of the house of Israel'. For some time the twelve had formed a sort of inner circle around Jesus. They enjoyed a close bond of friendship with him, having laboured in his company, which was a full-time learning experience. Now they were being sent as his envoys into the parts of Galilee where he himself had not gone. A glance at their backgrounds, which varied from fishermen, to tax collector to a Zealot revolutionary, was anything but impressive. These men would squabble among themselves about who was the greatest. Peter would deny all knowledge of his master. Judas would betray him. Thomas would doubt his resurrection and, when the crunch came, the rest would run away. We are left wondering could Jesus not have selected a better group? Why does he continue to risk his message to weak human beings, frail members of a fallen race, like ourselves? There is a sense of urgency in the sending forth of the twelve, which arises from Jesus' concern for the crowds, who are dejected and harassed like sheep without a shepherd. The heart of Christ was moved to pity and anguish at the sight of people his word had not yet reached. Their religious condition was pitiful, as they were living aimlessly without purpose or direction, and very much in need of encouragement. They were deprived of strong unselfish leadership and proper guidance. It was no small challenge for the apostles to continue the same work, which Jesus had begun. Their mission is a promise of God's continued care and concern for his people. We may be removed by some two thousand years from this gospel, picture but we can well ask, 'Has much changed?' Once we have rolled back the veneer of our creature comforts, as we look around we get the impression things are not all that different. People everywhere feel uneasy, vulnerable and confused. Some are driven to despair by the apparent absurdity of life. Many Christians are so deprived of proper guidance that they no longer seem to know what pathway to follow and what person to trust. In the midst of all our wealth and prosperity, there is an inner restlessness which disturbs us, a desert in the human heart that makes us search frantically for a purpose as to why we are here, and hunger for a meaning to our existence. There has to be more to life than what we have experienced of it. Everyone is thirsting for the good news that in God's eyes we are precious and that he cares and watches over us. In a world of pretence and lies that is becoming colder and less personal, the need to be reminded of God's steadfast love is greater and more urgent than ever before. The kingdom of God that Jesus announced was not some far-off dream that would happen in the distant future but a reality to be experienced in the bits and pieces that are part of everyday happenings. All our ordinary moments are means of entering into a more significant relationship with God who has invited us to open our eyes, to reach for the heavens, to develop a sense of reverence and dignity because we are all his children. If the gospel of Jesus Christ is to be kept alive and the good news that we matter to God, are precious and special in his sight, is to be announced in our age, then we must play our part. By virtue of our baptism, we are the distant descendants of those early followers of Christ and the essential character of our mission is the same. The work of the church is now in our hands. God wants all the earth to experience his love, and only with our co-operation can he continue his work. He invites us to be his witness in today's world, to promote his ideals and to reflect his concern for the poor and needy. Only with our words can he speak to people and only with our hearts and hands can his compassion reach them. We are all called upon to be an influence for good in our neighbourhood by being sensitive to the people with whom we work and live. God is standing at the door of our heart, waiting for an invitation to enter and bring into our being an infusion of his life-giving spirit.

Prayer of the Faithful

Celebrant: As God's holy people, called in different ways to spread the Good News, we now turn to God our Father and place our needs before him.

1. That our Holy Father and all who minister in the church may never tire of preaching Christ's message to the world.
   Lord, hear us.

2. That all who hold positions of responsibility may recognise God as the source of all authority, and strive to work with compassion and understanding.
   Lord, hear us.

3. We pray for farmers and all who work on the land. May they be blessed with favourable weather and gather an abundant harvest.
   Lord, hear us.

4. For those who are ill that they may experience the healing presence of Jesus through the kindness of those who take care of them.
   Lord, hear us.

5. We pray for our beloved dead who brought so many blessings into our lives. May they enjoy the peace of your kingdom.
   Lord, hear us.

Heavenly Father, the harvest of souls is abundant but the labourers are few. In your compassion hear us, and help us to take part with joy in the spreading of your message, through Christ, our Lord. Amen.

Twelfth Sunday in Ordinary Time

First Reading: Jeremiah 20:10-13; Second Reading: Romans 5:12-15
Gospel: Matthew 10:26-33

A word of encouragement does not cost a lot but it is described as the oxygen of the soul, and without it our enthusiasm and commitment slowly starve and sometimes die for want of appreciation. At those difficult moments when we are down in our luck and feel disheartened, encouragement is something we all need to help us think in new ways in order to make dreams and hopes stay alive. Three times in the course of this short gospel passage Jesus offers his apostles words of encouragement, telling them not to be afraid because the Lord's support will always be with them in moments of trouble. The apostles were about to embark on their very first mission as Christ's representatives and he highlights some of the dangers they will encounter. Jesus wants them to know that the Good News will not be welcome in every household, that opposition to their preaching will be inevitable, and that certain people will display open animosity to them. They must be ready for all kind of afflictions but will be sustained by knowing that evil, sin and death are not going to have the final word. No matter what people say or do to them, they should not be over concerned because to be a herald of the truth is never an easy task.

The lives of the early Christians, announcing the Good News of Jesus Christ, were lived against the backdrop of a pagan culture where there were no churches, no Sunday festivals no organised religious education and no church website. What is more, slavery, immorality, cruelty, suffering and the treatment of women as household chattels were commonplace. It was an age when travel was dangerous, communication was difficult, disease was rampant and most people were illiterate. Into this setting the apostles were sent, fired with the conviction that they were pioneers of a new humanity promoting a kingdom of life, light, goodness, justice and love. They puzzled their neighbours in the way that they remained loyal to Christ and ignored the lure of easy-going body-worshipping paganism. I mention this historical context as every day of our lives brings pressure on us to abandon our Christian principles. Many believers today talk about the difficulties of the times we live in and hearken back to a supposedly golden age of Christianity, as if there ever was an ideal environment for the announcing of the Christian faith. It is encouraging to realise that the Christian faith first took root and flourished in an atmosphere where it would have been impossible for any other message to survive.

The mission that was entrusted to the church at its very beginnings is the same task as is assigned to Christians of every age including our own. Apostles and disciples are people who have the truth of Christ written in their hearts and are able to make known the good news because God gives them that power through the Holy Spirit. The message given is that in God's eyes we have a worth and a value beyond counting. He loves us with an infinite love and values us so greatly that he sent his only Son to free us from our sin. His love can renew all things and the task of the faithful follower is to let this be known to people who feel far from God and are tempted to believe that there is no hope in their lives. The most effective way of proclaiming this good news is to live unashamedly by the values of Jesus Christ. In our world which is openly pagan we are often tempted to be quiet about our faith for fear of being ridiculed or laughed at. It takes moral courage to speak out, to stand up for what we know to be just and right in our hearts because for evil to triumph all that is required is that good people remain silent.

The message that is clearly heard in today's gospel is not to be afraid to be witnesses of the good news. Jesus is asking us to throw in our lot with him with the promise that he will see us through. Whether our fears are great or small with God's help we can find the courage to face them with calmness, firmness and determination. God does not ask us to come to him perfect. He works with us – fears and all – like clay in the hands of the potter. (Jer 18:6) We are not to fear what may happen tomorrow. The same loving Father who cares for us today will care for us tomorrow and everyday. He will shield us from suffering or give us the unfailing strength to bear it.

Prayer of the Faithful

Celebrant: Gathered together as a community to celebrate the mystery of our salvation, we turn now in prayer to God the Father confident in the care and concern he has for each of us.

1. For our Holy Father and all engaged in church ministry, that they may have the courage to bear witness to the demands of the gospel.
   Lord, hear us.

2. That the leaders of nations may be fearlessly committed, in a spirit of service, to their people.
   Lord, hear us.

3. For students sitting examinations at this time. May they give of their best efforts and receive the reward of their hard work.
   Lord, hear us.

4. For the sick and the disabled that they may experience the healing and comfort that only Christ can bring.
   Lord, hear us.

5. That those who have died recently may find eternal rest and happiness in heaven.
   Lord, hear us.

Heavenly Father, hear our prayers for the needs of all your people. May we never be afraid of professing our faith in you. We make our prayer through Christ, our Lord. Amen.

Thirteenth Sunday in Ordinary Time
First Reading: 2 Kings 4:8-11, 14-16;
Second Reading: Romans 6:3-4, 8-11; Gospel: Matthew 10:37-42

The French are noted for their lavish display of hospitality on the occasion of a wedding, and over the many years I spent in France as an emigrant chaplain, I was privileged to be present at several such gatherings. Coming home after one particular wedding I had the misfortune to find myself stranded at the roadside with a flat tyre. It was late at night and I was hours from home. A passing motorist came to my aid and not only helped me change the wheel but offered me lodgings for the night. Although I declined his offer, I was more than impressed with the gesture of hospitality – because to invite someone to be a guest in your home is a bit risky, especially if that person is a stranger. This happening came to mind as I read the quaint account of the welcome received by the prophet Elisha as he made his way to Shunem. The woman's kindness is rewarded by the gift of a son in her old age. It is a story which illustrates how in olden times hospitality in the East was regarded as a sacred duty. True hospitality was considered as the equivalent to receiving the Lord as a guest. Time and time again we are treated in the Bible to stories of how God, who is the master of disguise, appears to his servants in the very ordinary circumstances of daily living.

In this day and age hospitality is becoming increasingly difficult because we are part of a society where people are growing further apart and material things tend to be more important than neighbourliness. However, the happiest moments of our lives are the times when we offer and enjoy hospitality. It is the most beautiful gift we have to offer and although it costs time, energy, patience and understanding, it leaves us with pleasant memories. The strange thing about hospitality is that you may not find it where you expect it, but you know when you have been offered it because the occasion leaves agreeable memories.

Baptism should stamp into the lives of Christians a pattern of generous behaviour, which means that there ought to be no stranger or outcast in our midst. Everyone should feel welcome and at home in our company. In the gospel Christ calls us to reach out and welcome the stranger in our midst. This is not so much a keeping the door of our home open for strangers as having a welcoming heart for every person with whom we come in contact. The cup of cold water is an indication that the smallest act of kindness performed in a Christian manner will not go unnoticed. Once we reach out and share our lives with others, the rewards for trivial acts of generosity are enormous. The result will be a feeling of inner joy and fulfilment, which comes from doing the best we can in any given situation. In caring for others we allow the love of God to move through us. A random act of kindness blesses both the giver and receiver. We find tremendous joy and satisfaction in helping others as it results in comfort and healing, both for the giver and receiver. In every neighbourhood the less fortunate, the lonely and the rejected are crying out for a little recognition. Giving of our time in a kind and friendly way helps us to come to grips with inner selfishness and crack open the hard shell of our own indifference which tells us to remain aloof, to pass people by and not to get involved. The kind of welcome we extend to others is the surest measure of the quality of our Christian life and of what our faith means to us. If we really want to follow Jesus we cannot settle for the comfortable way of doing things but must be prepared for hardship. Every Sunday when we gather in church, Jesus welcomes us as his guests and invites us to break bread and share his life with us. He does this because he realises that the gift we are most in need of is his hospitality. What better gift can we leave to those coming after us than the breaking of bread and Christ's instruction to 'do this is memory of me'? It is a glimpse of the hospitality that awaits us when we arrive in our heavenly home.

Prayer of the Faithful

Celebrant: Mindful of God's steadfast love for humanity, we come now with open arms and lovingly place our petitions before him.

1. We pray for bishops, priests and religious that they may be true servants of the mysteries of Christ.
   Lord, hear us.

2. We pray that we will always reach out in kindness and generosity of heart to welcome the stranger in our midst.
   Lord, hear us.

3. May those who have become downhearted in life discover the generosity of God in the words and actions of those around them.
   Lord, hear us.

4. We remember all in our community who are sick at this time. May the Lord fill their hearts with love and compassion.
   Lord, hear us.

5. For all who have died. May the Lord welcome them into his kingdom of love and peace.
   Lord, hear us.

Heavenly Father, you are ever mindful of our needs and concerns. Open our hearts to offer you our love and service, through Christ, our Lord. Amen.

Fourteenth Sunday in Ordinary Time
First Reading: Zechariah 9:9-10;
Second Reading: Romans 8:9, 11-13; Gospel: Matthew 11:25-30

Jesus must have been exceptionally disappointed that the Pharisees and religious leaders, to whom he preached in his home region of Galilee, were not more receptive to his teaching. They had their own approach to life's problems and felt confident of having all the answers. Their failure to recognise that Jesus' message came from God, did not leave him disillusioned. He had come to realise, through the enthusiasm with which his preaching and teaching was received by ordinary people, the extent to which the religious expectations of the Pharisees had left them crushed and broken. Jesus entered the world of common folk who were without hope, and were not wanted or respected by their religious leaders. The practice of religion, instead of being a source of help and support for ordinary people, had been over-laden with stifling customs and burdens of strict observance that were impossible to fulfil. Jesus recognises their turmoil and confusion, releases them from the burden of the Pharisees and having given them the experience of his comforting presence, speaks those words of warmth and welcome: 'Come to me all you who labour and are overburdened and I will give you rest.'

While this consoling invitation offers support to all who are burdened and in need of salvation, Jesus acknowledges that following him will not be without problems. He is not offering us a free passage from life's crosses, but will be present as an understanding companion in troubled times, like a friend who comes along, listens to our sorrow, offers us consolation and gives us the strength to continue our journey refreshed. On our part it means putting our hand into the hand of God with childlike innocence and actively trusting in our heavenly father who has a plan for each person. In this gospel Christ seems to beckon us all to come to him and learn from his ways of gentleness and humility. These are qualities hard to come by in our stressed-filled modern society where it seems that power, possession and privilege offer a more comfortable living and are the hallmarks of a successful person. Large injections of humility are required before we come to realise that we are not lords and masters of the world in which we live, but only short-term trustees.

There are times when we find life difficult and depressing with no escape from tension. We stagger under our burdens, some of which we have brought on ourselves. Whatever their cause, they weigh us down. We feel worthless and, as we struggle to cope with them, often there seems to be no let-up or no way out. All of us have experience of this type of situation especially when a person close to us is seriously ill, or when a valued relationship has turned sour and comes to a bitter end. Or again, it may be that the death of a loved one has left us alone and broken hearted. In the midst of everything there is a need to remain strong and not to lose hope. When faced with such problems it is important to know where to look and who to turn to for comfort and support. In the gospel Jesus invites us to tranquillity and peace. He points us in his direction and invites us to unload our worries and difficulties unto his shoulders and turn to him for help and reassurance. This coming to Christ requires a movement of the heart in prayer. Through all the confusion and turmoil of life we need to know that Christ is always working in our lives even when situations appear to be hopeless. He has a special affection for ordinary people and with his help we can live lives worthy of our dignity. Letting go of our worries and allowing God to guide us is both a practical and powerful way of sustaining our spiritual, emotional and physical well being. God and life go together and it is important to keep both in the picture. Once we turn to God for strength we no longer become stressed about everyday matters. We experience an immediate sense of relief because God is in charge.

The compassionate voice of Jesus is heard once we are aware of his presence, and bring our anxieties to him with love and trust. Compassion involves the entering of another's pain in the deepest sense no matter how uncomfortable it may be. Jesus preached this message of compassion when he healed the sick, fed the hungry, welcomed the outcasts and forgave sinners. He expects his followers to do likewise. We offer Christ's compassion through our encouraging words, warm smile, listening ear and comforting presence.

Prayer of the Faithful

Celebrant: Conscious of Jesus' words 'Come to me all you who labour and I will give you rest', we humbly offer our prayers to God our Father.

1. For leaders of the church, that they may preach the Good News, which brings comfort to all who are heavily burdened.
   Lord, hear us.

2. Let us pray for those whose lives have been shattered by acts of violence in the home or community. May they find healing in the love offered by family and friends
   Lord, hear us.

3. We pray for ourselves, that we may be freed from all selfishness and become more aware of the needs of those less fortunate than we are.
   Lord, hear us.

4. May all those who are weighed down by sickness find comfort and healing in the compassion of those who care for them.
   Lord, hear us.

5. For the recently deceased who have gone before us in faith that they may be raised up on the last day.
   Lord, hear us.

Heavenly Father, your Son promised to give us rest when overburdened. Bless us as we strive to build your kingdom here on earth. We make our prayer through Christ, our Lord. Amen.

Fifteenth Sunday in Ordinary Time
First Reading: Isaiah 55:10-11; Second Reading: Romans 8:18-23
Gospel: Matthew 13:1-13

Parables are disturbing stories, specially designed to awaken hearts that have grown dull and ears that are hard of hearing. Sitting in a boat at the lakeshore, Jesus preached this gospel story to the crowd seated at the water's edge against a backdrop of fertile fields and rocky hillsides. He uses the experience of his countrymen who worked the land and knew all about rich soil, stony ground and scorching sun to convey this important message about spiritual growth. In Palestine sowing comes before ploughing. The planter sows the seed lavishly, scattering it through the stubble, and along stony pathways studded with thorny plants, rocks and briars knowing that some of it will fall in the most unwelcoming of places. When the sowing operation is completed the ground is then ploughed up and the growth of the seed depends on the quality of the soil it has come to rest in. After all this hard work the sower can do no more and must leave everything in the hands of mother nature, waiting patiently until reaping time and hoping that his labour will yield an abundant harvest.

Between watering, weeding, feeding and protecting from harsh winds and frosts any gardener will tell you that caring for plants is a fulltime occupation. If seedlings are to put down healthy roots that will push up strong shoots, they need as much caring as young children. There are no short cuts or quick fixes in the world of nature. Jesus tells us that it is no different in the all-important matters of the heart and spirit. The story prompts us to think of God as The Master Gardener who has sown the seed of his word on the earth and scattered the sign of his presence generously throughout creation. He even gives the most unlikely places the opportunity of receiving his word and responding to it. If God's presence goes unnoticed the problem is due to a lack of welcome on our part, either because we are not listening or our hearts are elsewhere. It is not because he is absent. The word of God will take root and bear fruit in our lives depending on the welcome we give it in our hearts.

There is a saying in the Bible that we will ultimately reap

what we sow. All of us, by the manner in which we live our lives, plant seeds for good or evil through the values we impart to our families. The word of God bears fruit not only when it is grown but also when it is shared and handed down. As we listen to this gospel we may well stand back and ask ourselves if our faith has deep roots and if our hearts are centred on God. Are we trying to live out in our daily lives the beliefs we claim to profess in church on Sunday morning? Maybe we have lost touch with ourselves and have a sense of running on empty, of something deep within us withering away because we have become choked with materialism and are no longer hungering for the things of the spirit! In our better moments we genuinely want to answer God's call but we get caught up in worldly activities that on the surface appear to be more profitable. The end result is a shortfall between what is expected of us by God and what we know to be true of ourselves. Many of us have grown accustomed to compromising our principles and have settled for superficial lives of comfort and pleasure. There are periods in our lives when we feel that there has been no growth at all.

The parable of the sower assures us that despite all the frustrations we may encounter as we go through life, the miracle of growth will take place. The grain, which is scattered by the heavenly sower, will yield a return out of all proportion to what was sown. God's kingdom will arrive and the result will be a bumper harvest. God's ways, though mysterious, are ultimately successful. The plan he has for all of us may not be to our liking. It may be extremely hard to accept, but in the end he will carry us on eagles' wings and lighten our load. God is our loving Father, our creator and our support. Our lives are special for he created us in his image and likeness. Life is a God-given gift to treasure and enjoy. Neither the power of evil nor the selfishness of the human heart will deter God's desire to fill the world with his bountiful presence. Our lives can be changed by calling on God to make his home in our hearts and asking him to nourish us with the bread of his word.

Prayer of the Faithful

Celebrant: Just as the sower scatters the seed in the hope that it will take root wherever it falls, we pray to God the Father asking him to lavish his blessings upon our lives.

1. Let us pray for the Holy Father, priests and religious that they may keep sowing the seed of faith, even when they see no signs of a return for their work.
   Lord, hear us.

2. For farmers who toil the land and prepare the crops, that they will experience a plentiful harvest.
   Lord, hear us.

3. We pray that parents, by their example and encouragement, may create an atmosphere in their homes that will make the Lord's call heard and heeded.
   Lord, hear us.

4. We pray for all who are sick or deeply troubled in mind and body. May they find comfort in Jesus who is the Way, the Truth and the Life.
   Lord, hear us.

5. We pray for all who died recently that they might find happiness forever in God's kingdom.
   Lord, hear us.

Heavenly Father, help us recognise the seed of your word at work in our lives. We make our prayer through Christ, our Lord. Amen.

Sixteenth Sunday in Ordinary Time
First Reading: Wisdom 12:13, 16-19;
Second reading: Romans 8:26-27; Gospel: Matthew 13:24-43

Any gardener knows that weeds never fail to appear, and keeping them at bay is a constant struggle and an uphill battle. They can arrive almost overnight, creeping across the soil and if left unchecked can choke new shoots and entangle delicate blossoms. Although they have their own wild beauty, weeds disturb and destroy the order of things and are the greatest threat to the life of young seedlings. Removing them is a delicate operation and requires skilful fingers, if the root system of young plants is not to be severed and destroyed.

Addressing a rural community who were familiar with the problems of sowing, growth and harvesting, Jesus tells the story of a farmer who discovers that poisonous weeds are growing among his wheat. What makes matters worse is that they are purposely planted there and the work of a neighbour who has a score to settle. This particularly malicious crime is aimed not only at endangering the entire crop but ruining the farmer financially. By the time the problem is spotted, the weeds are so intertwined with the roots of the wheat that there is nothing for it but to leave them there until they are separated at harvest time.

Jesus uses the familiar image of weeds in a field of wheat to convey his message about good and evil in our lives. Our world is far from perfect and none of us needs any convincing about the existence of evil as every day the media brings its own litany of bad news. Human frailty makes us aware that there are weeds in our own make up, and despite our good intentions we seem incapable of changing and of living the type of life we want to live. We hear so much about suffering, hatred, violence and death that we are left wondering has evil triumphed, is good in danger of being suffocated and has God's kingdom dissolved into nothingness? There tends to be so much emphasis on what makes colourful headlines that the good news is left unmentioned and goes unnoticed. It is there all the same in all the unspoken acts of kindness, in the offers of help to neighbours in need from people whose lives are genuinely committed to gospel values. Each one of us can count numerous individuals whose daily lives are grounded in compassionate love.

The gospel story acknowledges that good and evil are present in all walks of life, and that the search for a perfect church or a flawless society is an illusion. Although Christ has entered our world, the ways of sin and death are not entirely behind us. A dilemma that bothered the early church was how to explain that there were saints and sinners within its establishment. Some believed that the church should consist only of the select, the chosen few, and that those who did not measure up should be rooted out and firmly excluded. Such a rigid policy of expulsion made no allowance for the fact that God has the care of all in his heart. People can change and conversion is possible. Sometimes we get it wrong and can be too quick to judge some as saved and others as damned. A more enlightened response is to imitate the compassion of Jesus who did not isolate himself from a world of sinfulness or from men who did not respond to his message. He ate with sinners, preached to lost souls and cured those who were spiritually ill, but never sought to impose or enforce his way of life on others. Having compassion for the wayward, he was slow to condemn, as he was anxious to extend the greatest amount of love and understanding to his people. Jesus never said that his church would produce an instant change in human nature. That would only happen at harvest time, meanwhile the emphasis is on the co-existence of good and bad, side by side within the community. While we should sort through the weedy areas and dark crannies of our own lives in order to become better people who have learnt from our difficulties, as a church we are called to be open, inviting and forgiving to sinners, as was Christ.

An important spiritual lesson to be drawn from this gospel is that our God is not in a hurry and that his patience comes from a great understanding and love of us. His power is unlimited and his concern extends to all his creatures. We are invited in our own lives to imitate his mildness and leniency, and to develop that capacity of looking beyond appearances to see the best in others, believe the best about them and encourage the best from them.

Prayer of the Faithful

Celebrant: With trust and confidence we come before God the Father who is our rock of refuge and place before him our petitions.

1. We pray that the church may become a community of love where all are welcome and no person feels rejected.
   Lord, hear us.

2. Let us pray for those who suffer from depression or anxiety that they will come to know the love the Father has for them.
   Lord, hear us.

3. We pray that as a parish community we may recognise the goodness in each other, show charity to all we meet and refrain from judging the wayward.
   Lord, hear us.

4. We pray for those who have lost their way. May they find direction and courage through the power of Jesus, our Saviour.
   Lord, hear us.

5. We commend to the mercy of the Lord all who have died. May they rest in heavenly peace.
   Lord, hear us.

Heavenly Father, fill our hearts with love that we may serve you more fully by seeing to the needs of others. Help us to walk the path Jesus has asked us to follow. We make our prayer through Christ, our Lord. Amen.

Seventeenth Sunday in Ordinary Time
First Reading: 1 Kings 3:5, 7-12; Second Reading: Romans 8:28-30
Gospel: Matthew 13:44-52

Unlike most precious jewels, pearls are products of living creatures. They come from the ocean and are found in the shells of
oysters in the warmer seas of the world such as the
Mediterranean. In ancient times pearls were regarded as jewels
of prime value, and precious possessions of any kind were compared with them. The pearl business was brisk in the Middle
East and merchants were known to have spent several years and
crossed many seas searching for pearls of the right size.
Biologists tell us that pearls are only created as a result of the
oyster's shell being damaged and in danger of being penetrated
by tiny grains of sand. As a means of survival the oyster triggers
a defence mechanism exuding a powerful liquid secretion,
which hardens around the foreign body and plugs the gap in its
shell. It is to survive and defend itself against attack that the oyster forms one of the world's most precious jewels. In the gem
trade, the largest pearls are called paragons and they are the
products of severely damaged oysters. All this may seem far removed from the glittering elegance of a palatial ballroom but
without the damage and suffering endured by shellfish the
necks of wealthy women could never be adorned by pearls.

Jesus told stories that gave his followers an insight into life.
He compares the kingdom of God to a priceless pearl found
after a long search by a merchant who is so enthused by his discovery that he is willing to sell all his earthly belongings in order
to purchase it. Those who risk their whole fortune know the
value of their investment and searching for the kingdom of God
is no different. Drastic risks have to be taken and personal resources expended as its prize is worth more than all other possessions and interests put together. The point of the story is that
no sacrifice is too great, no price too high to pay for the timeless
treasure and precious pearl of the kingdom of heaven.

This is a practical invitation to put aside all the distractions
that can take the place of God in our hearts. It may be power,
possessions, prestige or the comforts of an easy life. While they
are important, if we overvalue them we devalue God. Nothing

in the world should take priority over our pursuit of God's kingdom. There is a pearl for everyone, and the price to be paid to acquire it is the ability to detach ourselves and walk away from what we cherish most without any regrets. What counts when we die is not the possessions we have acquired in life but the type of people we have become in the process of living. The pearl of great price is to be found in doing God's will which brings meaning, direction, happiness and peace into our own lives and in discovering this we find our true selves.

In the early days of the church many people became Christians at a great personal cost and died for the faith, which they regarded as a very precious gift. They had their priorities properly sorted out. The same cannot be said of our age. We find ourselves in a situation not unlike King Solomon who was faced with a choice between real needs and a multitude of competing wants. Each day we are bombarded with advertisements subtly confusing needs and wants, telling us what we have not got, promising us the good life and pointing out that the road to happiness is to be found in the abundance of possessions. Solomon could have requested anything he wanted but in succeeding King David, he was aware of his personal limitations. To face the challenge of leadership what he needed most was an understanding heart, which sought to do the will of God and his prayer for this was highly commended by the Lord.

As a Christian community we are surrounded by the blessings of God's kingdom. Our pathway through life is studded with the rich symbols of Baptism, Confirmation, Eucharist and other Christian sacraments. For the want of making space for God in prayer, they may have become treasures we have overlooked, taken for granted and failed to recognise. In this gospel Christ is pleading with us not to let our faith in the kingdom of God lie buried on the seabed. He is inviting us to open our eyes and become aware of the treasure each of us has received. We are being called to come back to God and to put Christ and his teaching first in our lives.

Prayer of the Faithful

Celebrant: Knowing that our heavenly Father in his wisdom provides for all our needs, with confidence we approach him with our petitions.

1. For our Holy Father and all who serve in the church, that inspired by the wisdom of the gospel they may remain strong in faith.
   Lord, hear us.

2. For all who serve in positions of authority, that they may use their gifts and talents for the common good.
   Lord, hear us.

3. For all who live in the darkness of despair that they may find comfort in Jesus Christ who is the pearl of great price.
   Lord, hear us.

4. Let us pray for those who are sick in mind or body. May this faith community support them in caring for their every need.
   Lord, hear us.

5. We pray for those who have died recently. May they find a home in Christ's kingdom of light, happiness and peace.
   Lord, hear us.

Heavenly Father, we offer you our prayers, those spoken on our lips and those echoing in the silence of our hearts. Help us to use your gifts wisely and to rejoice in the treasures of your love. We make our prayer through Christ, our Lord. Amen.

Eighteenth Sunday in Ordinary Time
First Reading: Isaiah 55:1-3; Second Reading: Romans 8:35, 37-39;
Gospel: Matthew 14:13-21

On receiving deeply upsetting news we are inclined to with-
draw into ourselves. We need time and space on our own to get
away from things in order to come to terms with the harsh reality
of what has happened. This was what Christ was doing on hearing of John the Baptist's death. There was nothing for it but to retreat to a quiet spot on the other side of the lake for a sharing in
sorrow and grief at the loss of a close friend. Seldom does life
work out as planned and when Jesus stepped ashore, an eager
crowd were already gathered there to meet him. With them
were the sick, the needy, those searching with confidence in
their hearts for comfort and assurance. Christ's compassion
knew no boundaries. He came to restore a broken world and
each human being counted. As he stood in their midst healing,
teaching and listening to their sorrows, those who heard his
words of comfort and support knew that he was deeply concerned with the individual and felt that he was addressing each
of them personally. It was one of those pleasant days that passed
all too quickly and as evening approached the crowd were feeling the pangs of hunger. As the only food available was five
loaves and two fishes the apostles wanted to send the crowd
away to fend for themselves in the surrounding villages. In contrast, Jesus astounded the apostles when he challenged them to
look beyond what was possible. They were to take practical
steps and feed the people out of their own resources. Even in the
empty spaces and hungry experiences of life, Christ shows us
that good things can happen.

We are all familiar with the gospel story of the multiplication
of the loaves and fishes. Catering for the five thousand families
at the lakeside was clearly a miraculous and marvellous event.
What happened that evening we shall never know, but out of
the five loaves of bread came physical nourishment for a multitude of people who returned to their homes satisfied and feeling
the better for their time spent in the company of Jesus. As we
take a closer look at the life of Jesus in the gospels, we see that
meals played a central part in his ministry. He ate with sinners,

compared the kingdom of heaven to a wedding feast in his parables, spent his last Thursday evening on earth sharing a meal
with his disciples and, after the resurrection, his followers gathered to break bread in the form of a meal-like ceremony, which
we call communion.

If we look closely at a meal we will see that it is something we
all need and have in common. Many of our best memories,
which are fun to recall, are of family meals on festive occasions
like Christmas or a wedding. Sharing a meal with others involves
slowing down, taking time out to engage them in conversation
and finding out what is happening in their lives. Meals are not
just about consuming food and banishing the twinge of hunger.
They also nurture the soul by offering enjoyment, providing
hospitality, creating friendships, developing relationships,
spawning community and in signalling reconciliation. It is often
said that we can never really be enemies with someone with
whom we have shared a meal. In the Israel of two thousand
years ago, sharing a meal was almost regarded as a sacred action
which demanded that the host put aside any resentment or ill
will towards his guests and treat them with the utmost courtesy.

The church has always regarded the miracle of the multiplication of the loaves and fishes as a sign pointing to the Eucharist.
Jesus wanted to feed his followers in a spiritual manner by
means of the Eucharist. The taking and breaking of bread, the
blessing and distributing of fish symbolised the Messiah sharing
a meal with his people, satisfying their human needs and providing them with nourishment for earthly and eternal life. The
deepest yearnings of the human heart can find fulfilment only in
God who is patiently guiding us through the shadows of this life
towards the glowing reality of heaven. In the celebration of the
Eucharist, Jesus comes to us as our pilgrim food in the form of
bread and wine and satisfies our hunger for all that is most precious in life. The Eucharist penetrates into the depth of our being
to renew us by healing the wounds of sin and pouring the life of
God into us. Those of us who have enough and plenty of ordinary food to eat and drink must realise our obligation to share
generously with those who are less well off.

Prayer of the Faithful

Celebrant: Gathered like the crowd in the gospel and hungry for the word of God, we turn in prayer to our Father who does not fail his people in their time of need.

1. We pray that the Holy Father, bishops of the church and ministers of the Eucharist may always be enriched by the treasure they bring to others.
   Lord, hear us.

2. For those who serve at the altar of God and those who prepare, decorate and beautify the church – may the Lord bless them for their dedication and devotion.
   Lord, hear us.

3. We pray for ourselves: may the Eucharist mould us into a welcoming and caring community.
   Lord, hear us.

4. Let us pray that all who carry the cross of sickness, may never lose courage but draw strength from Christ
   Lord, hear us.

5. May eternal light shine on those who have died, especially those who have no one to pray for them.
   Lord, hear us.

Heavenly Father, your Son Jesus took pity on the hungry and fed them. Help us to hear the cry of those who hunger in our world and respond with generosity and love. We make our prayer through Christ, our Lord. Amen.

Nineteenth Sunday in Ordinary Time

First Reading: 1 Kings 19:9.11-13; Second Reading: Romans 9:1-15; Gospel: Matthew 14:22-33

When a storm is raging, the sea can be a terrifying place. Like so many natural forces, we are powerless against its crashing walls of angry water. Can you imagine being tossed about in a fishing boat by huge waves dancing around like pyramids? No wonder the apostles were in a panic. They were terrified out of their minds. Never before had they known such fear. It was a night for an experienced hand on the helm, a sailor with a keen weather eye who could sense the squalls and the violent mood-swings of the furious gale. Matthew presents us with a dark and disturbing picture of drama on the Sea of Galilee. All hands are on deck as the fearful crew make their way ever so slowly through the darkness of the night. They are battling against severe headwinds and furious waves that threaten to engulf their frail craft. Late into the night, just as the storm is at its height, a ghost-like figure suddenly appears striding towards them over the troubled waters. When they hear the voice of Jesus telling them to have courage and not to be afraid, Peter jumps out of the boat, is all set to walk on the waters only to panic as he looks down at the waves swirling around his feet. The Lord comes quickly to his rescue, saves him from drowning and chides him for his lack of faith. When Jesus climbs into the boat the storm immediately abates.

One of the early Christian symbols of the church was of a boat with sails set making its way and violently tossed about on the seas of life. It represented the church beset by persecution, living through difficult times, going through troubled waters and feeling isolated, rudderless and abandoned by the Master. This gospel passage with its nautical image was written for a church with problems amazingly similar to our own, and its message is just as relevant in our age as it was in apostolic times. Have you noticed in the story how Christ being in the boat is a symbol of all being well in the church? In the midst of the turmoil of life it is recognising the presence of Christ in the boat, in the church, in our lives, which brings inner peace, calm reassurance and a renewal of hope.

The gospel is stating that there is little point in worrying ourselves unnecessarily about the present state of the church, which is being rocked by innumerable problems and unanswerable questions. Although it is going through rough waters it has experienced worse in times past. The last promise that Jesus made to his apostles before his departure from this world was that he would be with them 'even to the close of the age' (Matthew 28:20). The sea of life can be very intimidating, but what is of more immediate concern are the stormy waters in our own households. The dark blustering gales break hard upon us when a job is lost, an exam is failed, a relationship is ended or sickness comes our way. What do we do when a stormy marriage, straying children and a walking into the future with some dreaded disease lash us? When circumstances become too challenging, we are inclined to retreat from our responsibilities. Sometimes, like Peter, we make a brave start at facing what is wrong, take a few daring steps, then lose heart and sink beneath the weight of our worries. As we row upstream against the odds to reach our goal and arrive at our destination, we find that our morale is constantly taking a battering and our problems seem to block God out. When we are in such danger and sorely in need of reassurance and inner peace of mind, to know that Jesus is in the boat can make all the difference. At moments like this we need to appreciate that the Lord will walk towards us over troubled waters telling us not to be afraid and will help us to face each day with faith and courage.

For those among us who are distressed by the events and happenings in life this gospel has a welcome word of encouragement. It assures us that God is ever present, always available, speaking to us in our everyday happenings and he will do everything possible to give us support. Perhaps we need to take an honest look at our lives and to discover the reason why we no longer experience inner peace and joy. Maybe it is because we have taken our eyes off Jesus and have stopped conversing with him in prayer!

Prayer of the Faithful

Celebrant: As we struggle through the ups and downs of life, we place our prayers before God the Father confident that he will listen to our requests.

1. Let us pray for our Holy Father, the successor of Peter. Give him the power of the Lord's presence to direct him in the storms and crises that face the church.
   Lord, hear us.

2. Lord Jesus, you calmed the storm on the Sea of Galilee and brought your disciples safe to the shore. Strengthen the faith of all those who believe in you.
   Lord, hear us.

3. We remember all who face storms which threaten their peace and security. May the Lord restore calm to their troubled lives.
   Lord, hear us.

4. May those who are ill be strengthened by our prayers and comforted by those who visit them.
   Lord, hear us.

5. That the recently deceased, who have faithfully lived their lives for the Lord, may now experience the glory of his risen life.
   Lord, hear us.

Heavenly Father, in moments of uncertainty calm our fears so that we may enjoy the peace and unity of your kingdom. We make our prayer through Christ, our Lord. Amen.

Twentieth Sunday in Ordinary Time
First Reading: Isaiah 56:1, 6-7;
Second Reading: Romans 11:13-15, 29-32; Gospel: Matthew 15:21-28

One of the inevitable consequences of growing old is the experience of bouts of illness from time to time. They come in many forms and we learn to accept them as part of the human condition. When we recover and are back on our feet, such temporary setbacks help us to appreciate the good health that we enjoy but are inclined to take for granted. However, when sickness becomes a constant companion of young people, we find acceptance difficult to handle as we feel that it is not fair to be burdened down with ill health at such a tender age.

Our hearts go out in sympathy to the Canaanite woman who stops Jesus in his tracks by throwing herself at his feet, demanding his attention. She pleads with him to have mercy and cure her little girl who is possessed by a demon. Living on the borders of the Holy Land, it was likely that she had heard rumours of the healing powers of Jesus and his very appearance in the locality attracted her attention. Although the Canaanites were the traditional ancestral enemies of the Jews and a race whom the Israelites regarded as sinful, wicked and godless, she approaches Jesus in complete humility, without pretence and with a deep concern. It was her love for her daughter that drove her to overcome every barrier and to persist in any search that could heal her child. Falling on her knees, she kept pleading with Jesus and succeeded in capturing his attention. She created such a scene that the apostles implored him to give her what she wanted. They were eager to get rid of her because she was shouting after them and making a nuisance of herself. While the apostles saw her as a problem to be removed, Jesus regarded her as a person to be cared for. Persistence won the day for her words touched his heart and she got the cure that she requested.

We could do worse than to take a leaf out of the Canaanite woman's book. She was a person of great faith and her lively exchange of conversation with Jesus shows that she wouldn't take no for an answer. As is often the case, faith is found in abundance where we would least expect it. Although an outsider, nothing would stop her believing that Jesus could help her daughter. Even his turning a deaf ear to her request did not put her off. She even brushed aside his implied insult about eating the scraps of the house-dog. In approaching Jesus she left herself wide open for ridicule and rebuke as the rules of society decreed that being a woman she should have kept her distance. According to the law of the day Jesus should have had nothing to do with her. She was a pagan and he was a Jew. Yet she came in search of a cure in an incident that foreshadowed the breaking down of racial divides. Sometimes we need to realise that there are some breakthroughs and solutions that will not happen unless we are alone with the Lord in prayer.

There are many lessons that can be drawn from this gospel for the story is not specifically about Canaanites. The woman represents anyone who is despised, disliked or hated. Jesus constantly made the point that love is not exclusively for those who are near and dear to us. He proclaimed that we must welcome the stranger, have time for the marginalised and show acceptance towards those who differ from us in race and religion. There are many pathways to God, whose wish is that everyone should be saved and come to a knowledge of the truth. The gospel is all about building bridges between people and extending the hand of friendship to those who are on life's journey but are travelling on a different roadway than ourselves. We are being called to widen our horizons and to acknowledge an openness to God among those who are of a different background or social class to ourselves. Every person is made in the image and likeness of Christ and deserves to be treated with dignity and respect, no matter who they are or where they live. The gospel is a gentle reminder that we cannot possess God for ourselves, that he can never be the exclusive property of one particular group. God is always greater than our idea of him and refuses to be confined by our narrow view of things. There is no limit to his love and there is no point at which he says, 'This far and no further.'

Prayer of the Faithful

Celebrant: With confidence in God the Father, who rewarded the Canaanite woman by granting her request, we now place our prayers in his presence and seek his help.

1. We pray for the church throughout the world, that it may be a channel of God's mercy, peace and love.
   Lord, hear us.

2. We pray that, as a community of believers, we may not be divided by petty barriers of hatred and prejudice.
   Lord, hear us.

3. May we learn from the example of the Canaanite woman that all who seek favour from God, with sincerity of heart, will be heard.
   Lord, hear us.

4. Let us pray for the sick at home and in hospital that they may find strength and healing in the presence of Christ.
   Lord, hear us.

5. We pray for those members of our community who have come to the end of their earthly pilgrimage. May they rejoice forever in the Father's house.
   Lord, hear us.

Heavenly Father, give us the gift of a cheerful heart so that, like the Canaanite woman, we may turn to you in faith and love. We ask this through Christ, our Lord. Amen.

Twenty-First Sunday in Ordinary Time
First Reading: Isaiah 22:19-23; Second Reading: Romans 11:33-36
Gospel: Matthew 16:13-20

Caesarea Philippi was a town situated just north of Palestine, at
the summit of a huge cliff where Herod the Great had once built
a temple of gleaming marble in honour of the Greek God, Pan. It
was in this setting that Jesus paused to ask his disciples the most
enduring question of Christianity: 'Who do you say I am?' There
were many people in biblical times who had never met Jesus,
although they had heard others talk about and discuss his person.
His identity was shrouded in mystery and knowledgeable locals
were content to put him down as a self-appointed wandering
preacher. For over two years, the apostles had been in the company of Jesus as he journeyed through Palestine, observing his
works, listening to his preaching and witnessing his miracles.
Now Jesus was pushing their loyalty beyond idle speculation.
He was testing their personal commitment to his way of life by
asking them for a decision as to where they stood. There was no
doubt in Peter's mind as to whom Jesus was, and speaking on
behalf of the group he declared his conviction that Jesus was the
'Son of the living God'. In return for this magnificent expression
of faith Jesus appointed Peter as the foundation stone of a church
that would keep alive his work, outlast the Roman Empire and
continue preaching the good news until the end of time.

Peter must surely be rated as one of the most interesting
characters in the gospel. Before responding to Christ's call to
come and be a disciple, he was by trade a fisherman who was
prosperous enough to manage his own boat. While we imagine
him as physically large, rock-like and sturdy with a natural gift
for leadership, the gospel portrait of Peter is anything but flatter-
ing as it focuses upon the weak side of his character. He comes
across as a very unstable person who is tactless, impetuous and
hot-headed. On one occasion in a fit of enthusiasm he tried to
walk on water and almost drowned in the process. Gethsemane
found him asleep when he should have been watching and
praying with Christ. In Pilate's courtyard he buckled under
pressure from a servant girl and with foul-mouthed anger denied ever having known the Lord. But the moment the cock

crew he was reminded of his cowardly betrayal and broke down in tears. On more than one occasion the Lord had to challenge, rebuke and reprimand him severely. Another flaw in Peter's character was his racist attitude towards non-Jews. At Antioch, Paul confronted and publicly condemned him for his prejudice against the Gentiles when he stopped eating with them because of pressure from the Jewish establishment in Jerusalem.

Nevertheless, it was Peter whom Jesus chose to be the leader of his church. It is fascinating to watch the way that Christ dealt with and helped Peter become the man who was willing to give his life for him. His conversion did not take place overnight but came about gradually and in the face of numerous setbacks. We are left wondering what it was about Peter that attracted Jesus to him because by human standards he was a disastrous choice for the job, as he exhibited the faults and failings of most of us. Perhaps Christ chose Peter as the chief apostle to indicate that the church was a refuge for sinners. Being so often in the wrong made Peter realise that he had many shortcomings and needed to trust in the mercy of the Lord.

As we journey on our pilgrim way, Jesus asks us as a community of believers the pointed question, 'Who do you say that I am?' Our response will reveal much as to the kind of people we are and what we want from life. To acknowledge Jesus as the Son of the living God means that we see life differently and have a deep-seated conviction about Christ, which calls us to live in a particular way. This will be evident in the way we treat each other because when we offer shelter to the homeless or reach out to someone in need we encounter Jesus. It is a day to give thanks for being members of the church built upon the rock of Simon Peter. We can learn so much from Peter about our own relationship with Christ in the way we share his faults and failings and blow hot and cold in our loyalty. What we need to acquire is Peter's trust in the Master.

Prayer of the Faithful

Celebrant: As we reflect on the foundations of the church, we offer our prayers to God the Father for our own needs and the needs of the world.

1. We pray that the Holy Spirit may inspire our Holy Father as he continues the work of Peter in guiding the church through difficult times.
   Lord, hear us.

2. Let us pray for the church throughout the world that it may faithfully announce the message of the gospel to all peoples.
   Lord, hear us.

3. We pray for all believers, especially in times of trial. May they never lose sight of Christ as the cornerstone and foundation of their lives.
   Lord, hear us.

4. Let us pray for the sick, especially those who are in hospital. May they be strengthened by the love of Christ, shown in the compassion of those who care for them.
   Lord, hear us.

5. For those who died during the past week. May our prayers bring comfort and peace to those who grieve their loss.
   Lord, hear us.

Heavenly Father, help us to live lives of genuine holiness and dedicated service to the church. We make our prayer through Christ, our Lord. Amen.

Twenty-Second Sunday in Ordinary Time
First Reading: Jeremiah 20:7-9; Second Reading: Romans 12:1-2
Gospel: Matthew 16:21-27

One of the greatest myths of modern life is the notion that happiness is attainable and that more money, a bigger house, a new car and the latest designer fashion can satisfy the mysterious restlessness in our hearts. We long for a trouble free existence where everything runs smoothly and where there is comfort without effort, roses without thorns and happiness without tears. Pain and discomfort of any kind is something to be avoided at all costs. According to the received wisdom of our age, happiness is to be found in the avoidance of suffering and in the relentless pursuit of pleasure. There is a pill for every ill, and suffering is generally regarded as an affront to our pride because of the difficulty in penetrating its mystery and bringing it under our control. All this is a long way from the world of the gospel and a far cry from the culture in which our parents grew up. While it may appear that previous generations were all too willing to accept suffering as the will of God, at least they were aware that you cannot take the cross out of Christianity, any more than you can take the pain out of living. In the real world no one can be guaranteed an easy life and the teachings of Jesus offer no promise of this. Suffering is an unavoidable part of human existence and at some time or other most people have to deal with sadness, disappointment, a sense of failure and pain.

As Jesus turned to face Jerusalem, he made it quite clear to his followers that trouble and persecution were inevitable. He was setting his feet on the road that led to the cross along which he was to face hardship, suffer grievously at the hands of the elders, be put to death and rise up on the third day. Peter was so shocked at the idea of a suffering Messiah that he rubbished the very thought of it. He was not ready for the high price to be paid for discipleship as he felt that Christ could preach the truth without tears. Jesus' reaction to Peter is a rebuke that is sharp and devastating: 'Get behind me Satan.' Christ was so dedicated to the will of his Father that he would allow no earthly obstacle to be placed in his way. It is hard not to feel some sympathy for

Peter who, like ourselves, thought along conventional lines and failed to grasp the wider significance of God's plan.

No one needs to be told that pain and suffering are part of every life. Suffering is a mystery and there is nothing good about it. If not handled properly it can make us bitter, angry and spiteful. Sitting in a doctor's waiting room recently, my attention was drawn to a poster that read:

'Everybody hurts some time, and talking about it helps.'

There is no issue which torments the human mind more than the problem of pain, and people spend much time and exhaust their energy trying to figure it out. We would do well to remember that suffering was in the world since time began and long before Christianity arrived on the scene. What Christianity did was to give creative meaning and a redemptive quality to suffering.

The cross of Christ stands at the heart of our Christian belief and without it we have no faith. From his birth in a stable in Bethlehem until his cruel death by crucifixion on the Hill of Calvary, hardship and suffering were part of the life of Jesus. 'Christ did not come to explain away our sufferings or to remove them. He came to fill them with his presence,' wrote Paul Claudel. As we journey on our earthly pilgrimage, Jesus invites us to shoulder our cross, whatever form it may take, and follow in his footsteps. St Rose of Lima said: 'Apart from the cross there is no other ladder by which we may get to heaven.' Jesus calls us to see through the make-believe designer world of those who say we can live without hardship, to reach out to others in their pain and accept suffering in trust and confidence. Human suffering is never meaningless and can be both the measure of a person and the test of love and courage. Sometimes the trials that come our way can become a blessing if they help us see ourselves more clearly. We can not avoid the path of pain, but how we walk it makes all the difference.

Prayer of the Faithful

Celebrant: Called as prophets to bear witness to our faith, we bring all our needs before God the Father, confident of his loving care.

1. For all who are engaged in ministry within the church, that they may cheerfully accept the responsibility entrusted to them and grow in the service of God's people.
   Lord, hear us.

2. We pray for those who are suffering and heavily burdened. May they never forget that the Lord is with them in their struggle.
   Lord, hear us.

3. That those who find it difficult to forgive may, with God's help, be freed from the bonds of anger and resentment.
   Lord, hear us.

4. For the sick and the disabled that they may experience the healing comfort that only Christ can bring.
   Lord, hear us.

5. May our recently deceased receive the fullness of eternal life promised by Jesus to all who believe.
   Lord, hear us.

Heavenly Father, look with mercy on our feeble efforts. Give us the strength and courage necessary to model our lives according to the commands of your Son. We make our prayer through Christ, our Lord. Amen.

Twenty-Third Sunday in Ordinary Time
First Reading: Ezekiel 33:7-9; Second Reading: Romans 13:8-10
Gospel: Matthew 18:15-20

My childhood days were spent at the seaside. The coastline can be quite bleak in winter when the strand is strewn with seaweed after a storm. November stands out in my memory as the month when farmers arrived on the beach with their carts to gather the seaweed, which is an excellent fertiliser for a crop of early potatoes. It always amazed me the value a drift of seaweed assumed when it was coming ashore and up for grabs between neighbouring carts. Men who had an instinctive fear of the sea and a natural aversion to water would rush out up to their waists in freezing waves to claim the prize. The greedy eye sees far and with everybody looking for a full cartload many a full-blown row took place on the beach which left families at odds with one another. That was my early introduction to fall outs among neighbours and conflict in community.

As we listen to the words of Jesus in this challenging gospel about settling our differences and mending fences, our minds may wander to relationships that have gone wrong and turned sour in our own field of acquaintances. All of us are vulnerable, the strong as well as the weak. Maybe we are feeling the hurt and pain of a close friendship in tatters due to angry words or a betrayal. While we are left nursing our grievances, we forget what made us friends in the first place and precious memories of happy days are replaced by bitter thoughts of what caused the break-up. The sad reality in life is that most of our quarrels and conflicts are not with business institutions or church but with people with whom we come in contact on a regular basis. While a stranger can bruise us a friend can break us. Relationships are never free from disagreements but sadly some of us need go no further than our own immediate family to experience the havoc created by rows over the contents of a parent's will, a strip of land or a boundary fence. Sometimes, for good measure, children are drawn into the equation or, failing that, innocent mutual friends, as a test of their allegiance. Where there was once an atmosphere of friendship, joy and good cheer, there is now tension, coolness and frosty silence. All of us know people whose lives have stopped growing because they focused their energy on something that someone did to them five, ten or twenty years ago.

This gospel about conflict resolution is stressing the importance of compromise, of learning to give a little and to develop a
sense of proportion. It is telling us that rows and misunderstandings do take place and always will. We should do everything in our power to avoid such disagreements but when they
do happen, how we handle them is most important. A little honest talking about how we feel wronged often clears the air before
too much damage is done. With a bit of luck and good grace, we
should manage to get ourselves out of most neighbourly dis-
putes which might otherwise escalate into some unbearable
minefield. In the cool light of day, a boundary line may not be
worth disputing about with bitterness and acrimony. But if you
are in the thick of things and family or personal honour is at
stake, the whole issue becomes of immense significance and it is
so easy to let slip the dogs of war.

When we are feeling hurt and upset it is most important to
share our feelings with a faithful friend who will recognise the
sacredness of the confidence being placed in them. Their offer of
help and guidance with our problem should encourage us to
handle the situation with Christian dignity. Experience teaches
that keeping a dignified silence about what has happened is
preferable to airing the matter in public, as the latter course of
action leads to gossip which can cause more damage than the
original fault. The gospel ends by giving us the assurance that,
wherever we are gathered together as a community rooted in
prayer, Christ is present in our midst. In an age when religion
has become increasingly privatised, God calls us in communion
with him and one another. Prayer can change us, bringing about
reconciliation by making us more aware and sensitive to the
needs of others. In troubled times, when we pray for peace with
others, we raise our consciousness to our Christian calling as
peace-makers in our parishes, our homes and in our personal
relationships.

Prayer of the Faithful

Celebrant: Mindful of his many blessings, we approach God our Father in prayer and ask for an increase of his grace within our worshipping community.

1. We pray that church leaders may, like Ezekiel, be fearless in speaking the truth and giving witness in their lives to the words they proclaim.
   Lord, hear us.

2. May those in positions of authority always judge wisely and show compassionate understanding in their decisions.
   Lord, hear us.

3. As a new school year begins, we pray that teachers and students may never lose sight of Christ, as a model and inspiration.
   Lord, hear us.

4. May the sick, the aged and the housebound find God's comfort and consolation in the compassion of whose who care for them.
   Lord, hear us.

5. Let us pray for our beloved dead who are now free from the anxieties of life. May they enjoy everlasting peace.
   Lord, hear us.

Heavenly Father, help us to lead truly Christian lives. May we imitate your goodness and be sensitive to one another's needs. We make our prayer through Christ, our Lord. Amen.

Twenty-Fourth Sunday in Ordinary Time
First Reading: Sirach 27:30-28: 7; Second Reading: Romans 14:7-9
Gospel: Matthew 18:21-35

Listening to a *Sunday Sequence* broadcast on the subject of forgiveness some time back, my attention was taken by a mother whose son was brutally murdered. In the course of the interview she stated that, while she had pardoned her son's killer and written a letter of forgiveness to him in prison, she felt that she was still not at the stage where she was ready to meet him face to face. It brought to mind a saying by C. S. Lewis: 'Everyone says forgiveness is a lovely idea until he has something to forgive.' We would do well to acknowledge how difficult most of us find this challenge especially if our hurts and resentments run deep. When Peter questioned the Lord, 'How often must I forgive my brother if he wrongs me? As often as seven times?' he was more than surprised with the response: 'Not seven, I tell you, but seventy times seven' because he was well aware of the limit placed on forgiveness by Jewish tradition which stated that forgiveness was restricted to three times and on the fourth God punished. Peter's question and the response of Jesus shows the great void between human thinking and the ways of God. In any age Jesus' reply seems totally unrealistic because nobody forgives to such an extent and, at the end of the day, there comes a time when we must return kind for kind.

The story of the master who cancels without any fuss his servant's debt, who in his turn shows no mercy to a fellow servant but has him thrown into prison over a trifling sum, is not lost on us. Its message is made uncomfortably clear in the closing line of the gospel. 'That is how my heavenly father will deal with you unless you each forgive your brother from your heart.' The pardoning presence of the Lord in our own lives is dependent on us showing a similar spirit of forgiveness to those who have wronged us. Just as God shows us mercy and forgiveness we in our turn are expected to be merciful and forgiving to each other. This is a truth most of us who have our own personal enemies conveniently overlook. From our experience of life and work in community we are painfully aware that relationships are scarred with old hurts and strewn with broken friendships. Our immediate reaction when a trust is betrayed or a confidence is broken is to seek revenge. Each time we remember the injury our resentment increases and settling the score becomes our main objective. When we hold on to our hurts and nurse our grievances we unwittingly allow ourselves to become enslaved by them. A bitterness, which is left simmering for years, can eat away at the human heart, leaving us emotionally blocked, causing us to turn in on ourselves and to self-destruct. A failure to forgive usually results in the absence of inner peace, an erosion of self worth and a feeling of isolation.

At times like this the cross of Christ reminds us of the Saviour's boundless forgiveness. In spite of his own pain and suffering, Jesus stepped outside the cycle of violence and offered a heartfelt prayer to God for those who crucified him: 'Father, forgive them, for they do not know what they are doing.' Jesus forgave out of love – a love so great that it enabled him to move beyond the wrongs inflicted on him to express his affection for sinful humanity by offering all of us unexpected and undeserved forgiveness. 'For this is the glory of the good news in Christ – that while we were yet sinners, Christ died for us' (Romans 5:8). Children are wonderful examples of how the human spirit can move past the mistakes and hurts of yesterday in the way that they forgive themselves and others. They let go of the past and move forward to new growth and understanding.

As we are part of a chain of resentment and anger which stretches back to the time of Adam and Eve, this is a day for taking a look at our relationships with others to see how they can be improved or healed. We have hurt others and we have been hurt. Everyone inflicts wounds and everyone needs to be forgiven. We stand in need of forgiveness for the things we have done wrong, for the neglect we have shown and for our lack of compassion. Life is too short to be wasted on stoking the fires of resentment. Only when we have grasped the immense mercy of God in forgiving us our own sins can we truly offer forgiveness to those who have offended us.

Prayer of the Faithful

Celebrant: With renewed confidence in the loving forgiveness of God the Father, we turn to him in trust and make our prayer.

1. We pray that our Holy Father and all who preach the gospel may follow the example of Christ in sowing the seeds of forgiveness.
   Lord, hear us.

2. Let us pray for those who find it difficult to forgive because of the wrongs they have suffered. Give them hearts generous enough to let bygones be bygones.
   Lord, hear us.

3. We pray that families divided by bitterness and discord may find freedom of the heart in letting go of resentment.
   Lord, hear us.

4. That the old, the sick and the lonely may feel the warmth of Christ's healing love.
   Lord, hear us.

5. For those who have died recently, that they may enjoy the forgiveness of God and be united with him in total peace.
   Lord, hear us.

Heavenly Father, help us to love one another with a sincere heart and forgive one another, for you have forgiven so much through Christ, our Lord. Amen.

Twenty-Fifth Sunday in Ordinary Time

*First Reading: Isaiah 55:6-9; Second Reading: Philippians 1:2-24, 27
Gospel: Matthew 20:1-16*

When it comes to the harvesting of grapes, the weather is an all-important factor as it can make or break a vintage. The most crucial decision the vine grower has to make is when to start, because once the grapes are ripe they have to be gathered quickly before the crop rots or is spoilt by mildew. Even an overnight storm can bruise the grapes and cause havoc to the harvest. Grape picking is a short, snappy, hands-on operation and extra help is needed. In today's parable we can sense how anxious the owner of the vineyard is to have his grapes gathered before night falls and the weather changes. He goes to the marketplace at dawn and continues his search for hired hands throughout the day up until an hour before sunset. The normal daily payment was a Roman denarius and for the landless peasants in Galilee a day's wages in return for casual work in the heat of the sun was the difference between a family having food on the table or going to bed hungry. There is a real twist to the story when it comes to payment time. Those who have worked only one hour cannot believe their good fortune as the owner pays them a full day's wages. A full day's pay for one hour's work was beyond their wildest expectations. When the word gets out there is an air of expectation among those who have worked all day from dawn to dusk, sweating under the severe heat of the midday sun. However, their hopes are dashed as soon as they discover their wages to be no different from that of the latecomers. It all seems so bitterly unfair as they think they deserve better. Their disappointment is intense and they are furious at what they regard as a blatant injustice.

It is rather difficult to listen to this parable without asking the questions, 'Why did Jesus tell the story?' and 'What point was he trying to make?' No matter how we try to explain it, this is a gospel that seems to leave us with more questions than answers. Granted, the latecomers hired at the eleventh hour were not loafers, and were just not lucky enough to be in the right spot when the hiring took place, 'No one has hired us'. At the same time, we feel a certain amount of sympathy for the early arrivals who laboured all day long. Something in us says that they had justifiable grounds for complaint and, when you come right down to it, our sense of fairness is disturbed by this peculiar way of going about things. The sharp and unfeeling reply, 'Are you envious because I am generous?' does not help matters.

If we focus our attention on pay entitlements we lose out on the real and essential meaning of this parable. We are being invited to dig below the surface and look for a deeper message to this story because the gospel is not about the unemployment problem, economics, social justice, wage settlements or labour relations. It is about God whose eagerness to forgive our sins totally exceeds all limits. His love for us knows no bounds and his plan of salvation goes far beyond human imagining. All is grace and our presence in the Lord's vineyard is the result of his free gift of love. None of us can do enough on our own to merit entrance into his kingdom or to be entitled to its blessings. Everything is dependent on the mercy and generosity of God.

The Jews who were listening to this story were in no doubt that it was directed at them. Somehow they thought that as the chosen people they were in a privileged position and were justified in looking down on the Gentiles who were late arrivals to the good news about the kingdom of God. There is a message in it for regular church-goers and people who pride themselves on lifelong fidelity to the gospel, not to be looking over their shoulder at repentant sinners and expecting preferential treatment. The mercy of God the Father is far removed from the narrow mindedness and limitations imposed by our tunnel vision and rigid calculations. The true Christian will be so appreciative of God's generosity in his own life as not to be envious of others. God is constantly prising open our minds, shattering the shell of our security, inviting us to be adventurous and to go beyond the ordinary boundaries of thought to ponder new horizons in order to make our ways more like his. No one can listen to this parable without feeling that this is a way of thinking that is totally beyond us.

Prayer of the Faithful

Celebrant: Trusting that God our Father is near to all who call upon him, we place our prayers and petitions into his loving care.

1. That the leaders of the church may reach out with generosity and love to those who feel lost and abandoned.
   Lord, hear us.

2. That we may always be diligent in carrying out the duties for which we are paid.
   Lord, hear us.

3. May the unemployed in our community never lose faith in themselves because of their inability to find work.
   Lord, hear us.

4. That the sick and the suffering may be comforted by the compassion and understanding of family and friends.
   Lord, hear us.

5. Grant eternal rest to those who have died recently and bring comfort and peace to those who grieve their loss:
   Lord, hear us.

Heavenly Father, help us in the heat of the day to bear the burden of our struggles and to seek your will in all we do. We make our prayer through Christ, our Lord. Amen.

Twenty-Sixth Sunday in Ordinary Time
First reading: Ezekiel 18:25-28; Second Reading: Philippians 2:1-5
Gospel: Matthew 2:28-32
21:28-32

Taken at surface level, this short gospel story of the two sons seems to be nothing more than a typical scene from the ongoing tensions that arise in family life. The father wants some daily chores done in his vineyard and on giving orders to the first son is greeted with an outright refusal. He is the type of young man who gives the impression of being rude and confrontational because he blurts out the first thing that comes into his mind. Behind it all his heart is in the right place because, on reflection, he goes off and does what he is asked. The second son is more conscious of his image. He seems eager to please and does not disappoint the father with a bad answer but has not the slightest intention of showing up.

When first preached, Jesus addressed this parable to the chief priests and elders of the people during the week immediately preceding his crucifixion. The son who said 'Yes' represented Israel's religious leaders who were all smooth professionals. They had lost touch with their followers and their religion was now nothing more than an empty ceremonial show. When John the Baptist came preaching repentance they ignored his message. Their big mistake was to think that the law alone could save them while ignoring everything else that God was saying to them. The son who said 'No' but changed his mind stood for the Gentiles, tax-collectors and sinners who listened to the Baptist's preaching, put the past behind them and repented. The very idea of sinners and harlots entering the kingdom of God in their place was downright insulting and offensive to the Jewish religious leaders.

When we listen to this parable, there is always the temptation to view it as a condemnation of another people in another time, forgetting that whatever rebukes were addressed to them are also applicable to us. The kernel of this gospel is that faith runs deep into action and lip service is no service at all. Idle promises and half-hearted actions are worthless. What we profess to believe has no meaning if it is not translated into active commitment and a wholehearted response to Christ. With regard to the age in which we live, it is true to say that there never has been an era of so many words and so little sincerity. A great amount of suffering is brought into the lives of some married people by the inability or the unwillingness of their partners to keep their promises. The words 'I do', pronounced in front of the altar as a wedding vow, when not lived up to, can cause enormous suffering and unhappiness within the family circle. The other side of the coin is the security, peace, harmony and confident love evident in the family circle from an awareness of real commitment. Less dramatic forms of suffering caused by people not keeping their word are empty promises like 'The cheque is in the post' and 'I'll be there first thing in the morning.' Call it whatever you wish, it boils down to a betrayal of the truth, a giving of your word and not keeping it.

No matter who we are, all of us are guilty of leaving a trail of broken promises in our wake. What is more, promises can never replace performance and fine words are never a substitute for fine deeds. Our lives are rarely a clear-cut 'Yes' or 'No' to God and while we can change for the better it is good to be mindful that we can also change for the worse. The good news is that God makes allowances for our weakness and is ever willing to welcome us back after we have failed him. 'Turning back', 'facing the truth', 'finding ourselves' are everyday words for what the church calls repentance. All of us are still journeying towards conversion and while it is the key to the Christian life, for most people conversion is not a dramatic once-and-for-all event. It is more a daily turning away from selfish interests, from ourselves as the centre of our lives and a turning to God and our neighbour in the midst of everyday happenings. For each one of us our conversion will be unique, but we can be certain that when we put the past behind us and turn back to God with all our heart, that it will bring us lasting joy.

Prayer of the Faithful

Celebrant: Mindful that we do not journey alone in our struggle to become better people, we pray to God our Father for the needs of all the Christian community.

1. For our Holy Father and all who minister in the church that they will have the courage and strength to live up to the trust given them.
   Lord, hear us.

2. Lord, inspire artists, writers and composers to create works which draw us all closer to God.
   Lord, hear us.

3. For families in crisis: may they have the strength to work through their problems and stay centred in the Lord.
   Lord, hear us.

4. That all who suffer through illness, loneliness or depression may find comfort through the care shown to them.
   Lord, hear us.

5. For those in our parish who have died recently that they may enter into the fullness of life in God's heavenly kingdom.
   Lord, hear us.

Heavenly Father, increase your grace within us so that we may accept your will with sincere and generous hearts, through Christ, our Lord. Amen.

Twenty-Seventh Sunday in Ordinary Time
First Reading: Isaiah 5:1-7; Second Reading: Philippians 4: 6-9
Gospel: Matthew 21:33-43

As the majority of people in olden times were unable to read or write, the ancient art of story telling was very popular and invaluable in bringing a situation to life. Whenever an important message had to be conveyed people told a story about it, and sometimes put the words to music. The parable of Isaiah's vineyard with its sour grapes is in the form of a harvest love song that goes straight to the soul. We can imagine the prophet disguised as a street performer trying to capture the attention of Jews on their way to the temple to celebrate the gathering of the harvest. He sings lyrically about a vineyard that was lovingly cared for by its owner. Having gone to such lengths to ensure success, there is the heightened expectation of a bumper crop. Suddenly the joyful mood of the song switches to a lament about what went wrong because the outcome was a crop of sour grapes. The unexpected message of the song is plunged into the people's heart, for it turns out that Yahweh is the vineyard owner and the song is about Israel, his chosen people. They had received so much care and attention from him but in return had made a woefully inadequate response to his love.

In the gospel, Matthew the evangelist adds a new twist to this vineyard story by turning it into a potted history of the chosen people. In it he has God talking directly to the chief priests and elders of the people who were supposed to be in charge but had repeatedly stopped at nothing to lead the people astray. They had lost sight of what they were supposed to be doing. Instead of serving God faithfully they were neglectful of the orphan, the widow, the homeless and the hungry. The servants appointed to collect the produce are the succession of prophets sent to help them turn back to God. When challenged to mend their evil ways, they turned a deaf ear to these Holy Men and treated them badly. The son and heir, sent as a last resort, is none other than Jesus, God's only Son, whom they rejected and put to death outside the walls of Jerusalem. The chief priests and Pharisees who listened to this parable were furious when they realised that it was directed at them.

It would be a mistake to listen to this parable of the vineyard and let it flow past us as a story of rejection by a people in a different age. There is always the danger of thinking that it has no relevance for our time and is not applicable to our lives. This story of unrequited love is about the dealings of God with his people in every age and has a message for today. God is the landowner and the world we dwell in is his vineyard. For a few brief years we are tenants and have a lease over our lives, which is not our own property. To pretend otherwise and to maintain that we are not answerable for our actions is complete foolishness. The notion that we really own nothing, not even our lives or the material possessions that give us status may upset our pride but it just happens to be true.

In a world dominated by the internet, e-mail, and digital TV, it is important to reflect on the things that really matter in the eyes of God. Too often we find ourselves following the fashions and values of the culture around us and neglecting the things of the spirit. In our scramble to be happy and fulfilled we have become part of an age that is prepared to go to great lengths to exercise the body and educate the mind but neglect the soul which is the centre holding everything together. We are forever on the move, in search of meaning, contentment and a purpose to life but go looking for them in the wrong places. The readings make it clear that, as tenants in the Lord's vineyard there are demands placed on us. We are expected to yield a harvest of kind thoughts and good deeds. In order to become the very best people that we can be, we are challenged to give our minds and our hearts to spreading love, showing mercy, promoting justice and displaying forgiveness. It is a day to ask ourselves if we are caring for the weak and working for reconciliation. The essence of good living is achieved in doing the ordinary things of life well.

Prayer of the Faithful

Celebrant: Pondering on the gospel admonition of the need to bear fruit, we approach our heavenly Father and make these requests.

1. That the church leaders may be living examples of Christ's love and remain steadfast against the forces of evil and injustice in the world.
    Lord, hear us.

2. May we, as thankful people, open our hearts and avail of the peace of God, which is beyond all understanding.
    Lord, hear us.

3. That in our lives we may bear the fruits of love, forgiveness, justice and peace.
    Lord, hear us.

4. For all who suffer physical and emotional distress. May they find peace and healing through the care shown them.
    Lord, hear us.

5. Let us pray for those who have died in faith. May they rest in peace.
    Lord, hear us.

Heavenly Father, as we journey through life, may we always seek to your will, bearing witness worthy of our calling. We make our prayer through Christ, our Lord. Amen.

Twenty-Eighth Sunday in Ordinary Time
First Reading: Isaiah 25:6-10;
Second Reading: Philippians 4:12-14, 19-20; Gospel: Matthew 22:1-14

Weddings are very joyful occasions in family and community life. Preparations are always hectic. No matter how careful and meticulous the planning is, getting everything right is virtually impossible. There is no better way to create coolness in a long-standing friendship than to leave someone's name off the guest list. What is highly unusual about this gospel story is the snub given to the king with the blanket refusal of the invited guests to attend the royal wedding. They showed no interest and simply decided to do something else. An empty banquet hall would have spelt disaster on such a happy occasion, so to avoid embarrassment, the king sent his servants to the highways and byways and gathered in an unusual mixture of people to ensure that the reception was lively and full of conviviality. What ruins this otherwise consoling story is the king flying into an uncontrollable rage at the sight of a poor unfortunate, practically hauled off the street without a wedding garment, and who had no real sense of what was happening. Although clothing had a special significance in early Hebrew culture, there is more to this story than the importance of dress code at a wedding.

The popular image in the Bible for Paradise was a banquet or a royal wedding celebration where there would be an abundance of food, the finest of wines along with music, song and dance. The Jewish people dreamt of a future time when the Lord would right all wrongs, put an end to death and replace sorrow and suffering with unending joy and jubilation. Many of the great sayings of Jesus were about inviting people to feast at this banquet table and sharing in the life of the Lord. The good news is that beyond this present life, God has planned for us a great future of heavenly bliss and as a gracious host he hopes that everyone will come to his celebration. The guests first invited were the people of Israel but instead of being delighted they spurned the invitation and did not treat his offer seriously but regarded it with indifference and outright rejection. It is comforting to know that God's love for humankind is so great that he does not give up easily on his people. Just as the king in the gospel story sends invitation after invitation to his son's wedding banquet, God sent prophet after prophet to Israel warning them to repent and mend their ways but to no avail. The religious leaders, who should have known better, rejected them.

When we were baptised we were officially called to be members of God's kingdom and that special invitation was imprinted on our hearts. It was a time of grace-filled importance because it marked our spiritual birth. At baptism the spirit of God takes possession of us in a very special way, to direct and guide us in the footsteps of Christ. Accepting this invitation is not something we should treat lightly. It is not a matter of saying yes on one occasion and forgetting all about it but an ongoing process involving a constant and daily renewal of our commitment. Sharing in the banquet of the Lord requires us to respond to his love by living life according to his ways and building up his kingdom in the world around us. In our everyday lives we may not have the ability to do great things but we have the power to do good things. These challenges come to us every time we have an opportunity to make a house into a home by showing forgiveness or when we offer help to those in need and care for the aged and the housebound. The only suitable clothing that is acceptable in the presence of God is the garment which has been woven out of the kind and charitable acts we have performed for other people on a daily basis.

Every Sunday we assemble as a community to celebrate the Lord's eucharistic banquet, the centre from which all grace flows. With all our faults and shortcomings we bring to it the hopes, desires and longings to make God known and loved in a world that does not want to answer his invitation. One of the fruits of our weekly gathering should be an increase in charity among us and a drawing closer to our brothers and sisters, especially the weak and poor of our community. We are a hope-filled people, holding tomorrow in our hands, and with the help of God's grace will keep our eyes riveted on our eternal future.

Prayer of the Faithful

Celebrant: Trusting in the love of God the Father, who has invited us to the banquet of eternal life, we place the concerns of our hearts before him.

1. We pray that our Holy Father and all entrusted with church leadership will seek fresh ways of bringing the message of Christ into the world of today.
   Lord, hear us.

2. God's invitation is not to be treated lightly. May we realise that membership of the church is not a guarantee of salvation unless we change our lives and put on Christ.
   Lord, hear us.

3. That we respond to the love of God by continually wearing the wedding garment of repentance and good works given to us at baptism.
   Lord, hear us.

4. May all who are ill place their trust in Jesus, the Divine Healer, who brings comfort and peace to all who believe.
   Lord, hear us.

5. For those who have died that they may be rewarded with the gift of eternal life.
   Lord, hear us.

Heavenly Father, you so loved the world that you sent your only Son to die for us. Help us to appreciate the love you have shown us and to make it a reality in our lives. We make our prayer through Christ, our Lord. Amen.

Twenty-Ninth Sunday in Ordinary Time

First Reading: Isaiah 45:1, 4-6; Second Reading: Thessalonians 1:1-5
Gospel: Matthew 22:15-21

Now and again we are prone to lose the run of ourselves and need to be brought down to earth. When the agents of the chief priests and Scribes made a sly attempt to discredit Jesus with their trick question about whether taxes should be paid to Caesar, they certainly got their comeuppance. No doubt the problem was cleverly thought out by their legal experts as Roman taxation was a nagging issue about allegiance to a foreign power. For God fearing Jews the yearly tax levy was a hotly debated subject. What they wanted from Jesus was a rash statement in favour or in rejection of Roman rule. To make a comment on political loyalty was a no win situation which would leave him open to condoning Roman occupation of the Jewish homeland or rebelling against it. With quick-witted clarity Jesus side steps their clever ploy, treats their vindictive malice with the contempt it deserves, turns the tables on his opponents and silences them. His reply, based on the examination of a coin engraved with the Emperor's image, 'Render to Caesar the things that are Caesar's and to God the things that are God's' must undoubtedly rank as one of the most famous quotations of all times.

This incident in Our Lord's life brings up the critical question of the relationship between the secular and the spiritual, between the church and the state. While the principle laid down by Christ in the gospel is clear and unambiguous, its application in particular situations is quite another matter as it leaves unclear the dividing line between what belongs to Caesar and what belongs to God. We live in two worlds as citizens of earth and as heirs to a heavenly kingdom with obligations to both. Between them religion and politics are the very essence of life. Politics concerns how we live our mortal lives and religion our eternal lives. They do overlap, as God's people have never lived in a vacuum and the tension between human authority and divine authority is something we all have to face. No community can exist without politics and it is for us to see that the quality of life is improved by our active sharing and the making of our voices heard at local and at national level. Society is the better for having men and women in public life who are not afraid to stand up and be counted. We do well to remind ourselves that God is at work bringing about his kingdom and establishing his reign in both the secular and religious sphere of events. Our Christian duty is to participate in the political process at election time by casting our vote in an informed manner. It is wrong for a Christian to actively support a political regime, which is anti-Christian in its policy. The arrival of our yearly income tax bill is a reminder that as good citizens we are obliged in conscience to pay our taxes, obey laws made for the common good and at all costs avoid devious manoeuvrings. Without the revenue from taxes our state would not have the ability to provide transport, roads, police, hospital, educational and a host of other services, which we take for granted in the smooth running of society. Cheating on taxes is cheating one's neighbour and little different from outright theft. We can mistakenly imagine that 'business is business' and that our shady weekday commercial dealings have no bearing on the rest of our life. Nothing can be politically right which is morally wrong. The call of the gospel is to conscientious service and there should be no compartments of our lives that are sealed off from God. Our Sunday worship and weekday work must harmonise and blend together. The challenge facing all of us is to connect our faith humbly and honestly to our humdrum daily lives. This story forces us to look deeply within ourselves and reflect on what are we really giving back to God whose imprint we bear and in whose image we are fashioned. It is hoped that we will bring to our living something of the good which the prophet Micah talked of when he said what Yahweh required of us was, 'To act justly, to love tenderly and to walk humbly with our God' (Micah 6:6-8).

Prayer of the Faithful

Celebrant: With confidence we bring our hopes and needs before God the Father who is the source of all worldly power and authority.

1. That the leaders of the church, by word and example, may inspire us to seek the kingdom of God above all else in this life.
   Lord, hear us.

2. Let us pray for civil leaders who hold public office. May they openly and courageously recognise their dependence on God and never pass laws which are contrary to justice and peace.
   Lord, hear us.

3. We ask that world leaders may co-operate to bring peace to all nations which are estranged.
   Lord, hear us.

4. We ask the Lord to comfort the sick and strengthen all those who are weighed down by the burdens of life.
   Lord, hear us.

5. We pray that all those who died recently may enjoy the reward of everlasting life in heaven.
   Lord, hear us.

Heavenly Father, look kindly upon us and renew us in your love so that we may serve you generously and humbly through Christ, our Lord. Amen.

Thirtieth Sunday in Ordinary Time
First Reading: Exodus 22: 20 26;
Second Reading: Thessalonians 1:5-10; Gospel: Matthew 22:34-40

Love is an over-used and much maligned word in our vocabulary.
It is used to denote every kind of relationship from the loftiest
spiritual experience to the lowest forms of pornographic lust.
Love can raise us to the heights and also plunge us to the depths
of despair. Living in an age which bombards us through the
media about the importance of love, it may come as a surprise to
hear this gospel reading. It tells us that there can be no true love
without God's love and that all loving relationships must in
some way reflect the Creator's immense love for his people. In
olden times the Jewish people knew that love was the key to life
and that if they did not love they were missing out on life. This
gospel reading is so brief that we may be inclined to overlook its
importance. Here, Our Lord faces us fairly and squarely with
the two commandments which he describes as the greatest. Yet
we can never listen to its timeless words about the twofold command to love God and our neighbour without being aware of
the forcefulness of the demands placed upon us. We may well
wonder how we can possibly achieve the very high ideal of
loving God with heart and soul and mind.

Despite what the marketing people would have us believe,
the Beatles were right when they sang, 'Money can't buy you
love.' It isn't for sale, it can never be faked and there are no sub-
stitutes. God is to be found in every encounter where there is
true love and that life long journey towards him begins when we
show deeds of love for one another. Most of us have no problem
with loving God who is our maker and redeemer and who has
destined us for eternal salvation. The least we can do as imperfect
human beings is to express our gratitude for his great goodness
and unbounded love towards us in private prayer and public
worship. However we can not claim to give our hearts and
minds to God without loving the people around us and that is
precisely where the challenge lies. From time to time we all get
on one another's nerves but normally we find it easy to love our
friends as we choose them and they return our love. The same is
true of our family because ties of natural affection bond us to

them but it is loving our neighbour which can present us with problems. Showing love can be difficult when the people next door are downright inquisitive, their children's manners appalling, not to mention the persistent beggar or the workmate whose constant chatter we find irritating. The people who are most difficult to love are the ones who need love most and demand patience and understanding. More often that not these are the moments, the occasions when we meet and encounter God who is passing by.

Our Lord did not include the love of neighbour as an after-thought. God cares how we treat others and is anxious that we should short-change no one especially the weak, the powerless and the helpless, and often he looks for our love in the guise of one of these. Our neighbour is everyone from the highest born to the most lowly, from the nicest to the nastiest. How can we call ourselves Christians if we are continually out of sorts with our neighbours and refuse to have anything to do with them? Because our love for one another must mirror Jesus' love for us we can not claim to love God while ignoring the needs of those around us. If we make the love of God the guiding principle of our lives, our hearts will not harbour bitterness or prejudice against those who differ from us by race, religion, nationality or colour.

When the whistle is blown and our last breath is drawn we will be judged on how well we have loved. In particular on how much we have loved our children, the old, the poor, the mentally retarded and those looked upon as of no consequence. It is only when Christ's teaching of love is lived naturally that it takes hold and catches fire in society. If as Christians we were to take God seriously and give him everything, our impact on society would be immeasurable.

Prayer of the Faithful

Celebrant: Reflecting on the love of God the Father for his children, we humbly present our needs to him, confident that they will be answered according to his will.

1. May our Holy Father and the leaders of the church be instrumental in bringing people to a deeper knowledge and love of God.
    Lord, hear us.

2. That our parish community may realise that love is the heart of the law and that true love knows how to serve.
    Lord, hear us.

3. In our lives give us the grace to love tenderly, to act justly and to walk humbly with our God.
    Lord, hear us.

4. By the gentle touch of your Spirit help us to develop a deeper compassion for the sick and the elderly.
    Lord, hear us.

5. Grant eternal rest in your heavenly kingdom to our recently deceased.
    Lord, hear us.

Heavenly Father, you know our every need. Help us to deepen our faith in you and to be shining examples of your love. We make our prayer through Christ, our Lord. Amen.

Thirty-First Sunday in Ordinary Time
First Reading: Malaci 1:14-2:2;
Second reading: 1 Thessalonians 2:7-9; Gospel: Matthew 23:1-12

During the course of our lives, most of us are fortunate enough to meet people in whose company we feel valued and very much at home – a mother, a teacher, a best friend. These were the people who had always time for us and were a shoulder to lean upon while growing up. When we were feeling down they were always there to boost our confidence, and in good times or bad they shared our joys and our sorrows. Their humble lives of service were an inspiration to all those with whom they came in contact. Religion or faith was not something they talked about but was evident as a driving force in the way they accepted hardships and faced disappointments when God did not answer their heartfelt prayers. They are in our thoughts as we listen to the hard-hitting words of the gospel telling us that the benchmark of true greatness is humble service of one another. 'The greatest among you must be your servant.'

Tension and conflict are in the air as Jesus reminds us of the qualities demanded for leadership in the Christian community. He is openly angry at the conduct of the Scribes and Pharisees who have betrayed their sacred trust and his words leave no room for misunderstanding. These religious leaders paraded themselves as good upright and faithful people but this was only a façade because their actions branded them as hypocrites who said one thing and did another. They peddled their authority imposing impossible rules and regulations on ordinary people, which instead of setting hearts free to love God and neighbour made them feel inferior, sinful and laden down with guilt. Life for them was about capitalising on religion so as to make themselves feel important. Their search for power, privilege and prestige was misguided and as a result their prayers were a sham and a meaningless charade.

For all the advances made in the world since this gospel was first preached by Christ, human nature has not changed one iota and his words sound a warning for our own age. Hypocrisy is not a vice that is exclusive to the Pharisees but an ever present hazard and the point can be made that we do not differ all that much from them. Nobody is immune from its influence. The problem with hypocrisy is that while we can quickly spot it in others we find it difficult to recognise its echoes of deception in ourselves. We seem to have a fairly refined capacity for self-deception. Isn't it true that we are so concerned about what people might think of us that we are scared of the real truth being known about our shortcomings whatever they may be. In a society which places so much emphasis on creating the proper image and giving the right impression, we are all good at pretending and have come to place a lot of emphasis on externals. When the winning of human approval becomes the dominant feature in our lives we are in serious danger of losing our way. It is small wonder that the church of today has its fair share of churchgoers who fail to establish the connection between their Sunday worship and weekday work. Aren't we inclined to make religion something that is respectable, safe and secure but has little or no bearing on our everyday lives?

All of us in one way or another are invited as baptised Christians to exercise the role of leadership and accomplish something in the life of the church. The ultimate proof of sincerity is that our actions are seen to match our words so that we show the way to God by our example. We are called to be people of service rather than people of power. Our individual gifts and talents are not meant to be treated as personal possessions. They are to be accepted graciously and gratefully and used with generosity and humility for the good of everyone in the community. In one way or another we are all servants of the Lord and of each other. There should be no place for jealously or the craving of attention by showing off or trying to be important. Such behaviour is unworthy of the gospel and empties God's word of power and meaning. In our relationship with Jesus there is no room for pretence. He knows and loves us as we are and calls us to be a better people living the faith with love and generosity.

Prayer of the Faithful

Celebrant: As a pilgrim people seeking to love the Lord more fully, we offer our prayers and petitions to God the Father.

1. We pray for our Holy Father and the bishops of the church that they may be totally dedicated to their high calling of preaching the gospel.
   Lord, hear us.

2. May parents and teachers instruct those under their care by the good example of their lives.
   Lord, hear us.

3. May we always seek to do what is right and may God's word be a living power influencing our actions.
   Lord, hear us.

4. Look with compassion on, and ease the suffering of the old, the lonely and the sick.
   Lord, hear us.

5. For all the faithful departed that, having shared the cross of Christ, they may now share his glory.
   Lord, hear us.

Heavenly Father, you are full of love and understanding for your people in need. Deepen our faith so that we may always serve you with sincerity of heart. We make our prayer through Christ, our Lord. Amen.

Thirty-Second Sunday in Ordinary Time
First Reading: Wisdom 6: 12-16;
Second Reading: 1 Thessalonians 4:13-18; Gospel: Matthew 25:1-13

Jesus shared in every part of people's lives, visited homes, sat at tables, went to weddings and here we have him telling a story, which revolves around two groups of bridesmaids, in order to give us an illustration of what the kingdom of God is like. The wise bridesmaids were prepared for every eventuality and were ready with torches burning brightly for the arrival of the wedding party. In contrast, the foolish ones were completely lacking in foresight, made no provision for an emergency and found themselves without oil in their lamps. The shock ending sees them locked out and excluded from the wedding banquet.

This parable of the wise and foolish bridesmaids sounds puzzling to our ears. It may help us get a better grasp of its meaning if we regard oil as a symbol of repentance and good works, which keeps the lamp of our faith commitment burning brightly. The oil that runs out, causing the spark of faith within us to dim, points to our neglect of good works that in the course of our lifetime we should have performed and which we can not borrow or make good at this very late hour. We can't recapture the past nor go back in time to accomplish something we never started. Jesus was using this popular story to convey a serious message about the end of time – sometimes called the end of the world. He was stressing the vital importance of being ready and prepared to meet the Lord and not to take entry into his kingdom for granted.

The great issue emphasised in the parable is the proper use of time so that we are always alert, attentive and awake. 'Stay awake because you do not know either the day or the hour.' An old Celtic saying states that life is but a sigh between two mysteries, and from the womb to the tomb is a short journey no matter how many years we may get. There is a sense of urgency about life and the years allotted to us pose the challenge of being aware of what is going on around us. Time is a precious gift from God and yet we tend to live with little or no thought as to where we are journeying. We know that life is passing us by but we are so preoccupied with the business of making a living and the duties of family and work that only rarely is there time to actually live. Seldom do we create time to hear the voice of God in prayer and to allow eternal values to influence our actions. Only when we become aware of the spiritual do we discover the truth and meaning about life and its activities.

Perhaps it is an occasion to ask have we anything to show for life's opportunities which is never given anew? This gospel brings to mind a popular prayer card which carries the message, 'Any good thing I can do, any kindness I can show, let me do it now, for I shall not pass this way again.' It is easy to fall into a rut and become so immersed in day to day happenings that we put important things on the long finger and give them scant consideration. We forget that when a great opportunity knocks on the door of our life, its sound is no louder than a heartbeat and it is very easy to let it pass by. If we are not to be left with regrets there are things we may need to do or say in our lives right now. Very often words of praise, recognition, encouragement and appreciation are overdue on our part and remain unsaid for the want of a little sensitivity. To deprive a hard working colleague or family member of well-deserved praise and appreciation is to inflict an incurable wound on their self-esteem. It never hurts to say thanks and it does not cost a lot to tell our nearest how much we love them. Some things can not be purchased or borrowed. It is up to me to say the word of appreciation, to be the caring presence by visiting a friend who is lonely. There are moments, occasions, opportunities in all our lives and we can make good use of them and not let them pass. In this way we are awake and attentive to the presence of God in our surroundings. This gospel is about being prepared to meet the Lord today and everyday. We do this by keeping the lamp of Christ burning brightly with the oil of prayer, the love of our neighbour and acts of generosity towards the poor.

Prayer of the Faithful

Celebrant: In each of us there is a longing for happiness which can only be satisfied in the kingdom of God. We now pray to the Father for the grace necessary to arrive there safely.

1. Let us pray for our Holy Father and the bishops of the church that they may keep the lamp of faith burning brightly as they care for their flock with the love of Christ.
   Lord, hear us.

2. For a greater realisation of the closeness of God who comes to us in the brokenness of those with whom we live and work.
   Lord, hear us.

3. That we may live in a state of readiness for the coming of God's kingdom, remaining watchful but never fearful.
   Lord, hear us.

4. Let us pray for those who are ill, that God may ease their pain and heal their wounded spirits.
   Lord, hear us.

5. Let us pray for all those who have died in the hope of resurrection, that the Lord will welcome them into his presence.
   Lord, hear us.

Heavenly Father, listen to our petitions, which we offer in faith. Help us to grow in holiness as we wait in joyful hope for the coming of your kingdom. We make our prayer through Christ, our Lord. Amen.

Thirty-Third Sunday in Ordinary Time
First Reading: Proverbs 31:10-13, 19-20, 30-31;
Second Reading: 1 Thessalonians 4:13-18; Gospel: Matthew 25:14-30

There was a time when I used to feel annoyed at the treatment
meted out to the unfortunate fellow in the gospel story who
buried his talent in the ground. He seems to have drawn the short
straw because not only does he start with less than everyone else
but when called to account he gets dismissed for clinging over-
cautiously to his master's investment. Nevertheless, when we
realise that talents were the equivalent of a seventy-pound silver
bar, which has enormous purchasing power, it was a highly
irresponsible act to dig a hole in the ground and bury the talent
there for safe keeping. By no stretch of the imagination could he
be called an enterprising or industrious individual because there
was no attempt on his part to take advantage and make profitable use of the opportunity presented. The very least he could
have done was to make a minimal effort and earn interest on the
money by depositing it in the bank. Not much was required of
him, but the problem was he preferred to do nothing rather than
take a risk. His offloading of the blame with the excuse that he
was gripped with fear at the master's severe reputation is un-
acceptable.

We can be like this with our talents and leave them unused,
forgetting that we have a deep responsibility to make the best of
them. To spend a lifetime as a Christian and to end up with
nothing to show for the opportunities that came our way, and
failing to realise that we had something unique to offer, is to
have squandered our giftedness. No matter what our ability
level, we are to make demands on ourselves, to be creative and
attempt something worthwhile for the Lord. Above all, we are
to avoid settling for mediocrity and all types of inaction which
amount to a negative response to our calling. If we use the gifts
we have received, they will flourish and grow, but if we keep
them hidden they will be of no use to ourselves or anyone else.

This parable is a gentle reminder of the abundance of our
capabilities, and challenges us to use them in the service of God
who is interested in what we make of our lives. Jesus calls us to
be people of faith who are up and doing rather than people of

fear. Sooner or later we have to decide – either to listen to those fears that stifle life and growth, or to listen to the voice of Jesus, which tells us to take risks and move forward. No giftedness can survive the blight of neglect. Even a musical note will lose its sweet romance and become a wasted treasure unless it is exercised frequently. How can we say we are making the most of our potential as children of God if we are not using wisely the gifts we have been given?

Sometimes we feel inadequate and harbour secret longings to have someone else's qualities. At moments of low self-esteem we compare ourselves unfavourably with prominent and leading lights in the local community and wish we were more accomplished. We are disappointed that our lifestyle lacks sparkle and is all too crushingly boring. Nobody notices us, we are not a dazzling success, we fail to impress or have clout. It is easy to forget that God has blessed us with our own special talents, gifts of nature and grace, which can touch the lives of others. What really counts are the small commonplace things, as is indicated by the lady in the first reading who won recognition for her family by being a good wife and mother in a happy home. Everything we do out of love is important. Much of our life is spent assessing our self-worth in an effort to discover what our particular talents are. It will be more for some and less for others but they are all precious. Perhaps I am a good listener and a thoughtful person who by my presence and compassion make weak people strong and sad people happy. The drab routine of everyday can be enhanced by the loving attention we bring to our work. The gospel is an encouragement to do our best and make the most of our giftedness. It is a reminder that our mission is to grow in the grace of God. All of us have been given natural abilities that can blossom, and we will be judged on the daily use we have made of them in the service of Christ and our neighbour.

Prayer of the Faithful

Celebrant: Gathered together as a believing community, we acknowledge the greatness of God our Father, who is the giver of all good gifts, by reverently making our petitions to him.

1. We pray for our Holy Father and the bishops of the church that, enriched by the Holy Spirit, they may direct the flock entrusted to them in the ways of truth and love.
   Lord, hear us.

2. For a deeper appreciation of the importance of our ordinary lives and for a realisation of how the love of God can flow from our little acts of kindness.
   Lord, hear us.

3. That we may always make the best of the opportunities that come our way in the service of Christ and our neighbour.
   Lord, hear us.

4. For doctors, nurses and those in the caring professions who use their gifts to bring Christ's love and compassion to the poor, the lonely, the sick and the imprisoned.
   Lord, hear us.

5. Grant eternal rest in your kingdom to our deceased relatives and friends.
   Lord, hear us.

Heavenly Father, help us to remain faithful in the small things of life so that we may be trusted with greater when we come into your kingdom. We make our prayer through Christ, our Lord. Amen.

Thirty-Fourth Sunday in Ordinary Time
The Feast of Christ the King
First Reading: Ezekiel 34:11-12, 15-17;
Second Reading: 1 Corinthians 15:20-26, 28
Gospel: Matthew 25:31-46

Some sixty miles to the west of Paris stands the magnificent cathedral of Chartres, a masterpiece of twelfth-century gothic architecture. Above the southern doorway of the cathedral, hewn and chiselled in stone, is depicted a marvellous portrayal of today's gospel – Christ the King in judgement. Crushed under his feet are the serpent and the lion, the twin symbols of evil and corrupt power. On Christ's left, filing off to damnation and on his right, to salvation, are two groups of people. The tour guide will draw your attention to the smiles of happiness on the faces of those on the right in contrast with the expressions of despair of those going left. And he will remark, 'Notice that the figures on the right are those of ordinary people while those on the left represent society figures – one has a crown, another a mitre, then there's a banker clasping his money bag, a monk with tonsured hair, and the fifth has a book of the law in his hand ...'

With the death of nature in evidence all around us, this Feast of Christ the King brings the liturgical year to an end. Matthew set the scene with a pictorial impression of the last judgement. This immense picture painted in a few words gives a powerful image of Christ assuming the mantle of leadership as a true shepherd and acclaimed as Lord of all creation. 'When the Son of man comes in his glory escorted by all the angels, then he will take his seat on his throne of glory.' The thought of the day of the Lord, when we come face to face with Christ to give an account of our lives is daunting and awesome. In the moment of judgement everyone will be held responsible for the conduct of their lives and every act will carry the burden of consequence. There will be no pretence or escaping the scrutiny of the Almighty who looks at nothing except the human heart. All masks will be removed, all hypocrisy exposed and we will be shown up for what we really are. The human conscience will stand naked before Christ and there will be a full revelation of the truth. The yardstick for judgement will not be the knowledge we have gained, the fame we have won, the wealth we have acquired or the quality of our lives, but our performance or neglect of the corporal works of mercy. Who we are on the inside will determine the value of our worth. The power that created us will either look upon us as his friend or fail to recognise us as belonging to his household. Everything will depend on how we have treated the poor and downtrodden, for the Christ who holds the destiny of the universe in his hands has chosen to make himself known through the pangs of the hungry and the loneliness of the outcast. Our eternal destiny will hinge on our lives being cloaked in the deeds of human kindness. We touch God by respecting the brokenness of others in their confusion and pain.

This gospel encourages us to reflect seriously on how we are in our relationships with one another or have fallen short in serving Christ in the least important members of our community. We may well ask what are we doing to further God's kingdom on earth. When was the last time we visited an ageing parent, a lonely neighbour or closed our eyes to someone in need of help? How often after rows have we held the moral high ground and stripped a friend of their dignity because we were reluctant to offer forgiveness? I had plenty of food but was hungry for the nourishment of a little recognition and a word of encouragement to boost my self-confidence when the going was difficult and all I got from you was a sour look. We meet Christ in the beggar stretching out his hand for alms, in the refugee who is made feel unwelcome on our streets, in those afflicted with Aids and in the victims of civil strife.

From the all round expressions of wonder, surprise, shock and amazement at the unexpectedness of the judgement, 'Lord when did we see you hungry and feed you etc?', it is obvious that the virtuous served God without realising it and the condemned were unaware that they had slighted his presence. It could happen that on Judgement Day many churchgoers might make the discovery that they never knew Christ at all. If we were to live out our responsibilities and show God to the world as best we can, there are areas of our own conduct where change is necessary. What will give shape and meaning to our lives on earth are the joining together of love of God and love of neighbour.

Prayer of the Faithful

Celebrant: As a pilgrim people making our way to the kingdom of God the Father, we make our prayers with a sincere heart.

1. For the spiritual leaders of the church that, like the Good Shepherd, they may guide and protect us as we journey towards the kingdom of God.
   Lord, hear us.

2. We pray for those who hold positions of power. May they be inspired in their leadership and decision-making by the example of Christ the King.
   Lord, hear us.

3. For those oppressed by forces beyond their control – hostages, prisoners, the poor, the persecuted and the lonely.
   Lord, in their weakness may they know your strength.
   Lord, hear us.

4. That those bearing the cross of an incurable illness may receive the strength and comfort of God's peace.
   Lord, hear us.

5. We pray for those who have died in Christ. May the Lord receive them with love and mercy into his heavenly kingdom.
   Lord, hear us.

Heavenly Father, your goodness is visible to us in Jesus, who is both Shepherd and King. When we are called to give an account of our lives, may we be found pleasing to you. We make our prayer through Christ, our Lord. Amen.

The Feast of St Patrick

First Reading: Jeremiah 1:4-9; Second Reading: Acts 13:46-49
Gospel: Luke 10:1-12, 17-20

We are fortunate that Patrick, the patron of Ireland, is one of the few saints who left an autobiographical sketch of his life. While we do not know what he looked like, we can get an idea of his life and character from his writings. In his *Confession*, written in his declining years as his last will and testament by which he wished to be remembered, we have the story of his soul. Here, he speaks of himself with truth and dignity and hides nothing. It even gives an account of how, in his youth, he turned away from God and did not keep his commandments.

Patrick was born into a well-to-do Christian family in Roman Britain around 390 AD. His father was a deacon and his grandfather a priest. When he was 16 years old an Irish raiding party in search of slaves seized him from his father's house near the village of Bannavem Taburniae, somewhere on the coast of Wales. They bustled the terrified teenager into one of their ships and on arrival in Ireland Patrick spent six years herding swine on the Antrim hills. We can scarcely imagine the hardship and misery of those years in captivity. The pain and loneliness of exile must have eaten into his young heart, since he had been torn from his family, deprived of his freedom and left cold, hungry and exhausted on a bleak Irish mountainside. Instead of becoming bitter at his misfortune, Patrick tells us that, in his distress, he turned earnestly to God whom he had neglected in his youth. He discovered the importance of prayer and as he learned to walk with God, developed a love for the things of the spirit with increasing frequency. 'My spirit was stirred up so that in a single day I prayed as often as a hundred times and as many more by night, even when I was in the woods or on the mountain. I rose before the dawn to pray ... in times of snow, frost and rain' is how he describes his growth in prayer.

When the opportunity arose, he made good his escape to a new and better life and sometime later, began his studies for the priesthood as a mature student. According to himself, he was a slow learner but managed to persevere and kept at his studies. He admits to a lack of sophistication and is humble enough to tell us that he was despised by many of his contemporaries as being rustic, ignorant, unlearned and unfit for high office and church missionary work. 'I blush with shame and positively quake at exposing my own incompetence.' The wonder of it all was the call he received in a dream to return to Ireland and make his home there. We can hardly blame his relatives and close friends who advised him against such a foolhardy decision in view of the hardship that he had received. Surely he was well rid of that violent people who had treated him so badly! There were more pleasant pastures to exercise his vocation. To return to the land of his imprisonment must have been a grim and difficult turning point. 'But one night he heard in a dream the voice of the Irish, those by the wood of Voclut near the western sea. We ask you boy to come and walk once more among us. I was cut to the very heart, so I woke up.' Patrick was a man of great forgiveness and out of love for Christ, he came back to share his life with those who had wronged him.

His return to Ireland was symbolised by his lighting of the first Pascal Fire on the hill of Slane and the breaking of the rule of the pagan high king of Tara. He took on the Druids and destroyed their idols. After an apostolate that lasted thirty years Patrick died in Ireland leaving behind a people whose conversion from paganism to Christianity bordered on the miraculous. As Patrick looked back on the work of his life he saw with absolute clarity that his success was due to God's power at work in him. He was a born orator who never lost the run of himself and spoke the plain language of our forefathers. He shared their life and felt for their problems. The grace of God was with him and the people were converted because they found Christ in him. They received his preaching with enthusiasm. As we call to mind the story of Patrick's robust faith, we realise that the rich heritage that is ours is due in no small measure to the succeeding generations who saw that it took a firm hold. Our present challenge is to seek new ways of expressing that faith meaningfully in the nooks and crannies of our everyday living.

Prayer of the Faithful

Celebrant: United with the generations of believers that have gone before us in the faith of St Patrick, we make our prayer to God the Father.

1. We pray for the leaders of our church that, like St Patrick, they may be loving shepherds of the flock entrusted to them.
   Lord, hear us.

2. That Irish people at home and abroad may proclaim their faith and spread the kingdom of God.
   Lord, hear us.

3. That all Irish people may recognise their common Christian heritage and grow in mutual understanding.
   Lord, hear us.

4. For those seriously ill that, through the intercession of St Patrick, they may find strength and consolation in the cross of Jesus.
   Lord, hear us.

5. We commend to God's loving mercy all who died and for whom we have been asked to pray.
   Lord, hear us.

Heavenly Father, listen to our prayers on this festival of St Patrick. Open our hearts to share with others the riches of faith we have received. We make our prayer through Christ, our Lord. Amen.

The Feast of Saint Joseph
First Reading: 2 Samuel 7:4-5, 12-14, 16
Second Reading: Romans 4:13, 16-18, 22
Gospel: Matthew 1:16, 18-21, 24

The ability of the Spanish to let their hair down and party is unrivalled and legendary. They do this in the festivals they hold throughout the year. Sundays are a great day for these celebrations especially if the happening has got to do with the honouring of a saint's feast day. Valencia holds the annual festival of *Las Fallas* in March to honour St Joseph. It takes the form of a procession parading through the streets to the main square in front of the basilica where flowers are offered in a ceremony to Our Lady of the Helpless. After this, a gigantic bonfire is set alight to the sounds of music and dance. The night of the 19th March is called *La Nit del Foc* (Night of Fire) ending as it does in a huge fireworks display. The tradition has been traced back as far as the Middle Ages when carpenters, to honour their patron saint, used to make a bonfire with the wood shavings from their workshop floors.

It seems strange that St Joseph is so often depicted as a grandfatherly figure, sombre, bearded and old and as if to support this image, there is the tradition of praying to him for a happy death. After all, he was the only person called upon as a support and help to Mary in bringing up her son. Most of our knowledge of St Joseph comes from the opening chapters of the gospels of St Luke and St Matthew where we learn that he was a carpenter who lived in Nazareth and a descendant of King David. At the time of the annunciation, he was betrothed to Mary and it came as a great shock for him to find that she was carrying a child that was not his. Being a man of honour, his integrity would not allow him to give his name to a child he did not know, so he felt the right thing to do was to break his ties. At the last moment, when he had his mind made up to carry out his plan, an angel appeared in a dream and told him not to be afraid to take Mary as his wife, because the Holy Spirit conceived the child. Although Joseph did not understand, he humbly accepted that God had chosen him for this special role.

He proved himself to be a faithful foster-father and took

Mary with him to Bethlehem for the census. While they were there, Mary gave birth to Jesus in a stable. No Christmas crib is complete without the figure of Joseph who, with fatherly care, watched over the infant. His silent background presence is testimony of God's great love for all the poor, humble and just people down through the ages who, like Joseph, are quietly faithful to God in good times and in bad. Aside from his virtues as a man of faith, it is also worthwhile to note Joseph's status as a poor, working man. At the presentation of the child Jesus in the temple, he and Mary could only afford to sacrifice doves. His stamina was truly tested during the flight into Egypt to escape the slaughter of the innocents, after being warned in a dream of Herod's murderous intentions. Joseph is last mentioned in St Luke's gospel at the finding of the child Jesus in the Temple (Lk 2:42). He remains in the gospel text in a mocking gesture, which is a reminder of the humble origins of Jesus. 'Can anything good come from Nazareth?' 'Is this not Jesus, the carpenter's son?'

It is almost certain that Joseph died before Jesus began his public life, as on Good Friday just before the crucifixion Jesus entrusted Mary to the care of the apostle John. In spite of his important supporting role in the mystery of redemption – as husband of Mary and foster-father and guardian of the Child Jesus – not a single word is attributed to him in the New Testament. Joseph was a man who gave everything in the service of Christ. His example gives us courage to face problems in a similar spirit and to go on believing when all seems hopeless. We are asked to receive Christ as freely and as fully into our hearts as he did and to make the major decisions of our lives based on the faith given to us by God. If we believe like Joseph there is no limit to what God can achieve in our own very ordinary lives.

Prayer of the Faithful

Celebrant: Like Joseph, an upright man of honour, we place our trust in God the Father as we make our prayer for our own needs and those of the church.

1. We pray that the leaders of the church may set an example of committed service to the poor and the marginalised in society.
    Lord, hear us.

2. For carpenters and for all who work with their hands, that they may earn their living through skill and enjoyment of their trade.
    Lord, hear us.

3. That our homes may always be places where we may feel free to share our troubles and anxieties as well as our hopes and joys.
    Lord, hear us.

4. We pray for the sick of our community that the warmth of the love which they receive from family members may be a comfort to them in their illness.
    Lord, hear us.

5. For the dying, that St Joseph may console them in their last hours.
    Lord, hear us.

Heavenly Father, you have given us St Joseph as an example of unselfish, loving service to others. Help us to live in peace and harmony with each other. We make our prayer through Christ, our Lord. Amen.

Solemnity of Ss Peter and Paul
First Reading: Acts 12:1-11; Second Reading: Timothy 4:5-8, 17-18
Gospel: Matthew 16:13-19

In an age when the teachings of the church are being brought
into question, it is good on this feastday to recall that the Lord
built his church on the lives of these two men of faith. The
solemnity of St Peter, our leader in faith, and St Paul, its fearless
preacher, reminds us that everything we know and believe
comes to us from the apostles. Apart from them, we would have
nothing upon which to base our Christian faith. Peter was a fisherman with little or no schooling who was blissfully unaware of
the greater world outside of Galilee. He first came into contact
with Jesus by the lakeshore where his boat served as the master's
earliest pulpit. By nature, Peter was full of energy and impetuous.
There was nothing cunning about him. If he had a strong feeling
about something he let you know it. The gospels go to great
lengths to stress his weakness, fear and failures. He had a tendency
to act first and think later. Peter was never at his best when relying on his own imagined strengths. When he thought he could
walk on water, he sank. At the Last Supper he made the bold
claim to remain a loyal and steadfast friend of Christ to the bitter
end. 'Even though they all fall away, I will not.' However, before
the night was over, a servant girl taunted him and his courage
ran out. He denied knowing Jesus three times. We can sense his
appalling misery as the Lord gazed at him with a look of love
after sentence had been passed. Despite betraying Jesus in his
hour of need, Peter experiences forgiveness and is given the
wonderful task of looking after all the people whom Jesus loved.
One thing Peter teaches us is the importance of getting up and
rejoining the struggle, no matter how often we may fall. Often
failure can be the finger of God pointing the way, awakening
within us an awareness of our own helplessness.

We first meet Paul in the Acts of the Apostles, on the edge of
a murderous mob that is stoning St Stephen to death. Luke notes
that Paul approved of this terrible deed. Paul was a champion of
the old Jewish religion as well as a fierce foe of the Christian way
of life. He even scoured the countryside in search of Christians
to persecute. It was on one such escapade to Damascus that his

life was suddenly changed. A flash of light threw him to the ground and he heard Jesus calling out, 'Why are you persecuting me?' At that moment he realised that to persecute Christians was to persecute the Messiah who somehow lived in the members of his church. From this time forward Paul was driven to share the exciting truth of the gospel. He was a man of action driven on by the all-consuming love of Christ. His missionary journeys implanting the seeds of the gospel brought him through much of the Mediterranean world. His strategy of first approaching the local synagogue frequently provoked violent persecution and resulted in him being beaten, stoned and imprisoned. The outcome was that he found himself preaching to Gentile audiences who proved to be more receptive to his message. Paul was difficult to live with and seemed to have a charisma for causing controversy wherever he went. Apparently, you could have Paul or peace but it was difficult to have both. As well as being a missionary he was an intellectual who thought through the great questions of faith.

While they lived, Peter and Paul had different parts to play in the life of the new church. They were different in background and character and represented two different approaches, which will forever be in creative tension with one another. Peter moved slowly to new ideas. It was his view that things should remain as Jesus left them and it took nothing less than a special vision before he understood that the Gentiles were to enter the church on equal terms with the chosen people. Paul's idea was that there were issues that Jesus hadn't dealt with but which could not be ignored. There will always be a creative tension between the Peters and the Pauls if the gospel message is to find expression in a changing world. Both apostles were martyred in Rome under the persecution of the Emperor Nero. According to tradition, Paul was beheaded and Peter met his end by stretching his hands out on a cross, just as his master had done. Both may have been scapegoats for the torching of the city of Rome but they did light a fire that has not gone out. For this we give thanks.

Prayer of the Faithful

Celebrant: We bring our prayers and petitions to the Father with the faith of Peter the fisherman and Paul the missionary, on whom the church is built.

1. We pray for our Holy Father, the successor of St Peter, that he may continue to carry out his office with wisdom and love.
   Lord, hear us.

2. For the countries where Christ is not known, that missionaries with the zeal of Paul may bring them the good news of where the Lord can be found.
   Lord, hear us.

3. May we, as a believing community, lead others to Christ by the quality of our Christian lives.
   Lord, hear us.

4. That the faith and hope of the sick may be firmly anchored in Christ, who is the resurrection and the life.
   Lord, hear us.

5. We ask you, Lord, to raise from the dead all those dear to us who died with faith and hope in the resurrection.
   Lord, hear us.

Father in heaven, hear the prayers of your church and help us to lead lives founded on the faith and courage of Peter and Paul. We make this prayer through Christ, our Lord. Amen.

Assumption of the Blessed Virgin Mary
First Reading: Apocalypse 1:19, 12:1-6, 10
Second Reading: 1 Corinthians 15:20-26; Gospel: Luke: 39-56

The Assumption of Mary into heaven is a belief so deeply embedded into our Catholic consciousness that it may come as a surprise to learn that devotion to Mary, as we know it today, took a long time to develop in the church. For almost five centuries at the beginning of the life of the church, Mary had no special place of honour accorded to her. There were pressing problems that the early church had to face, with the result that Mary's place of prominence in the story of salvation did not receive the recognition that it deserved. Yet from the beginning it was always part of pious belief that someone so holy as Mary, who played such an unique role in God's plan of salvation, was preserved without blemish from worldly corruption and at her death was taken up body and soul into heaven to enjoy eternal life in the company of her Son. Christians did not believe that her body could disintegrate in the normal way after death, but went immediately from an earthly state to a heavenly state without passing through decay. This does not mean Mary did not die, but on completing her earthly life, she was assumed body and soul into heaven as its Queen.

The gospel describes the story of Mary going cross-country to visit her cousin Elizabeth who, late in life, is expecting a child. We see her with the loving tender heart of a woman who has the common touch and never considers herself better than anyone else. As soon as she enters Zechariah's house and gives her greeting, Elizabeth is filled with the Holy Spirit. The child in her womb leaps with joy in recognition of the presence of the unborn Jesus in their midst. Elizabeth, bursting with delight, proclaims the meaning of what has happened and acknowledges how honoured she feels at having a visit from the mother of the Lord. Mary's response of thanksgiving embraces a vision of her future role in the plan of salvation, indicating how, as a woman, she has been treasuring extraordinary secrets of God within her heart. As a pious Jewish woman, with a humble and an unspectacular life of faith, her deepest longing is to respond completely to God's intimate calling. She acknowledges that, all that is hers, is the result of God's mercy and favour. Because she is nothing other than poor, weak and needy, the Almighty is able to do great things for her. She shows us that the condition for receiving God's gifts is to be totally at his service while having an awareness and recognition of our nothingness without him. Mary's hymn of praise is a constant reminder that the standards and values of this world do not last. She is a voice for the powerless and a refuge for all who are oppressed and in difficulty.

In our troubled and unsettled world, the Feast of the Assumption gives us great hope as it directs our hearts and minds beyond the cares and concerns of the present moment. We believe that what God has done for Mary, he will do for us, if we are open and responsive to his word. Her presence in heaven is the promise that someday we will be there in her company. Our faith and our hope will not be disappointed but will be fulfilled beyond all expectations as we struggle to win the same victory that she now enjoys. On this mid-August feast, Mary gives us a message of comfort and reassurance as we make our journey through life. She reminds us, when our lives are crisscrossed with pain, suffering and the same blend of ups and downs as was hers, that the human story does not end in the darkness of the grave because God wants to share his life with us.

The Assumption is a joyful reminder of our heavenly Mother and of the special place she holds in God's plan for our redemption. Her final destination points out where we are going. While we are making life's journey, Mary watches over us, protects us, inspires hope and encourages us to be bearers of the joyful news, as she was, when she visited her cousin Elizabeth. Just as she provided the child Jesus with a safe dwelling place within her own body, she invites us to make a safe space for him in our own lives. In this way, the glory of the Lord will shine forth for all to see.

Prayer of the Faithful

Celebrant: Today the church celebrates the glory of the Virgin Mary's assumption into heaven. As we draw inspiration from her life, we place our prayers before God our Father.

1. May all who hold positions of responsibility in the church joyfully announce the assumption of Mary into heaven as a sign of hope and comfort in a despairing world.
   Lord, hear us.

2. We pray that, following the example of Mary, all mothers may make their homes dwelling places of love and holiness.
   Lord, hear us.

3. That those who have lost their way in life may turn for refuge to Mary, the Mother of Mercy.
   Lord, hear us.

4. May those who are sick and in sorrow find comfort and assurance in praying to Mary.
   Lord, hear us.

5. We pray that our beloved dead may enjoy eternal happiness in the company of Mary and all the saints.
   Lord, hear us.

Heavenly Father, as we celebrate the assumption fill our hearts with gladness and grant that, through Mary's intercession, we may come safely to eternal happiness. We ask this through Christ, our Lord. Amen.

The Feast of All Saints

First Reading: Apocalypse 7:2-4, 9-14; Second Reading: 1 John 3:1-3
Gospel: Matthew 5:1-12

Even though we live in a culture that has little or no regard for religion, people are still captivated by the spiritual. Most of us possess an instinctive ability to recognise heroic sanctity when we see it. Holiness manages to strike a chord in every human heart. There are people from our own neighbourhood and from our own community who make a profound impression upon our behaviour and whose good example influences us greatly. They infuse their surrounds with the spirit of the gospel. Their very manner of living gives us a glimpse of the face of Christ. We have all come into contact with people like that, who live their faith in a non-spectacular manner. The raw material of their holiness is rearing a family, coping with the cares of everyday and struggling to make ends meet. Like ourselves, they experience the trials of growing up and the tensions of living with others as well as all the normal difficulties and uncertainties that arise from time to time.

This feastday is a reminder that the true company of saints is far more numerous than the list of those who have been formally canonised. As scripture says, 'They form part of the great cloud of witnesses.' All Saints Day is also a recognition by the church that in our search for God we need the help of human faces and firm friends whose lives are steeped in genuine holiness. They inspire us to take a higher path. We belong to a community that has been graced by a history of goodness and fidelity to the gospel. Most of us have had the good fortune to have our lives blessed by the edifying example of such people. Their guidance encourages us and spurs us on, telling us that our future is with God because we are already his children. This is a day for us to thank the Lord for the enriching presence of these wonderful people in our midst. They blaze a trail for others to follow.

It is also an occasion to remember those who are no longer with us but have gone home to God. They are now enjoying eternal bliss. We rejoice in their good fortune and celebrate the excellence of their single-hearted commitment to the Saviour's will. It has been our privilege to experience the particular texture of their lives.

We thank God for their whispered prayers, which have uplifted us all. Few of them held important positions and even went unnoticed in their local communities. No book tells their story; no Christian calendar announces their name. They applied themselves seriously to the task of being human, understanding their vocation in the profound sense that God made us to know, love and serve him in this world and to be happy with him in the next. The one thing they all had in common despite their different personalities was their faith. The lives of these ordinary people were totally dedicated to God who was their stronghold. No matter what was their status, they acknowledged their total dependence on their maker. Their greatest lesson to us is that they never ceased trying to live holy lives. They show us the way and point out the path that we have to travel.

The last thing most people want to be known as is a saint. We have the mistaken notion that being a saint is beyond our grasp. Yet, sainthood is our calling. Sanctity is open to everyone. We have a destiny that invites us here and now to lead holy lives so that we can enjoy God's life and love in eternity. Heaven is within our reach and holiness of life is not for the privileged few but what God demands of all of us. What is more, we don't have to step outside the doors of our homes to start growing in holiness. Holiness is about bringing the spirit of Christ into our lives. The command of Jesus, 'Be perfect as your heavenly Father is perfect', is addressed to everyone and is an invitation to reflect something of the holiness of God himself. Cardinal Suhard put it well when he said, 'To be a saint means to live in such a way that one's life would not make sense if God did not exist.' As we honour the vast army of God's friends, in the same breath we ask God's favour, that where they are now, we too may be in the future. We pray that this will be our feastday as well.

Prayer of the Faithful

Celebrant: Inspired and encouraged by the example of all the saints who have shown us that, in spite of our weaknesses, it is possible to live like Christ, we turn to God our Father with all our needs.

1. That all Christians, striving to live the Beatitudes, may enrich the world with their compassion and love.
   Lord, hear us.

2. That we may come to realise we are all called to sainthood in our lives by the ordinary everyday acts of kindness and charity.
   Lord, hear us.

3. Give courage and confidence to parents and teachers who guide young people in the ways of holiness and so help to build God's kingdom among the next generation.
   Lord, hear us.

4. May those who mourn find comfort in Christ, who binds up hearts that are broken.
   Lord, hear us.

5. In the silence of our hearts we commend to God those deceased relatives and friends whose very manner of living gave us a glimpse of the face of Christ.
   Lord, hear us.

Heavenly Father, we give thanks for your love and rejoice in the communion of saints. We make our prayer through Christ, our Lord. Amen.

The Feast of All Souls

*First Reading: Isaiah 25:6-9; Second Reading: Romans 5: 5 -11;
Gospel: Matthew 25:1-13*

There is an Old Italian proverb that says: 'Love makes time pass, but time also makes love pass.' It is sometimes used with reference to the Holy Souls. In November the splendour of the year crumbles, the autumn leaves fall to the ground and are blown across fields and forest. The bare branches of the trees are etched across grey and wintry skies. Nature seems to be preaching a silent sermon about beauty fading and everything disappearing. God alone remains. In such a setting November is well suited as the month we set aside to remember, in a special way, those who have gone before us and with whom we lovingly passed happy times. Memories come flooding back of those who have been with us until recently; those who were alive last year; those who shared our childhood days; those who were the constant companions of our early adult years and with whom we met the adventures and responsibilities of life; those who gave us their love and received our own; those who gave us life. Each has carved a special place within the hearts of the people who knew them. Some of them left a name behind them, so that their praises are still sung. Others have left no memory and disappeared as though they had not existed. An elderly lady with no relatives told me recently that one of her greatest fears is that there will be no one to pray for her after she leaves this world: 'I am the last of the family – there will be nobody coming behind me to pray for me,' she lamented. Holy Souls Day is an attempt to reach out in faith to those who have connections with us but who have died. As we visit churches and cemeteries we bring with us in our hearts unanswered questions as to what life is all about. Why are we here? Where did we come from? Where are we going? Is there a hereafter? While the meaning to life is often elusive, the meaning of death, humanly speaking, is beyond our grasp. Is it the final and absolute end of our existence and the mocking conclusion to life on earth? Where are our dead? What shall become of them? Shall we ever see them again? It is precisely because of the reality of death that we must take life seriously. The ground of Christian hope is not that we can communicate with the dead

200

but that Jesus died, rose from the dead and will come again in glory. The person of faith believes we are precious and that death is our passing over into God. It tells us that even now we must start living as men and women of another world.

From the earliest times there has been a solidly based belief among the faithful of praying for the Holy Souls. Some among us may wonder why we pray for the dead. Does it make any sense? What possible difference can our prayers make to a person who has died? We pray for the dead for the same reason as we pray for anything. We all need to pray and praying does us good and helps us. Prayer for the dead comforts and consoles the living. Praying for our dead loved ones can help heal our relationship with them. When a close friend dies it can happen that we experience a certain amount of guilt because, being human, we have had a less than perfect relationship with the deceased. There is much unfinished business between us. There may have been disagreements that never were fully resolved. Maybe there is anger at having been left to do the nursing of an elderly parent while the brother got the property! And all of us have experienced the pain of letting go of a loved one and giving them back to God. In praying for the dead we help purify those unresolved matters that caused us bitter pain. The truth is that a vital stream of life continues to flow between our loved ones and us, even beyond death. Since death washes many things clean, the forgiveness we pray for is purer and the healing more enduring. Ever since the first Good Friday on the Hill of Calvary when the repentant thief on the cross cried out for mercy, 'Jesus, remember me when you come into your kingdom', the prayerful remembering of people has been at the heart of the church. We shall all meet again. Those who live in the Lord never see each other for the last time.

Prayer of the Faithful

Celebrant: Confident that nothing in life or death can separate us from the love of our heavenly Father, we make our prayer of petition to him.

1. We pray for church leaders and all Christian people that they may never tire of preaching the resurrection from the dead and the life of the world to come.
   Lord, hear us.

2. We pray for our deceased family and friends whom we remember throughout the month of November. May God gather them into his kingdom.
   Lord, hear us.

3. We remember all those who have died and have no one to pray for them. May the Lord, in his mercy, hold their names close to his heart.
   Lord, hear us.

4. For all who are filled with sorrow over the death of a loved one, that God may wipe away their tears and grant them peace.
   Lord, hear us.

5. For those in their last agony. As they share the passion of Christ, so may they come to share his crown of glory in heaven.
   Lord, hear us.

Heavenly Father, hear the prayers we make for our departed brothers and sisters. As we continue on our pilgrim way, may we prepare for a happy death by a holy life and so attain the glory of the resurrection. We make our prayer through Christ, our Lord. Amen.

The Immaculate Conception

First Reading: Genesis 3:9-15, 20
Second Reading: Ephesians 1:3-6, 11-12; Gospel: Luke 1:26-38

As part of our prelude to Christmas we celebrate The Feast of the Immaculate Conception, an event which occurred a full generation before the birth of Christ. It recalls the beautiful origins of Mary, born of the wedded union of her parents Anne and Joachim who lived in the remote hillside village of Nazareth. Mary was brought up as an ordinary girl and faced the same problems of life with its daily dullness of routine, which was the lot of all the people in the locality. By our standards Mary would have lead an uncomplicated life and like any other girl would have spent hours doing the usual household chores such as fanning the fire, preparing meals and fetching water from the well. Her parents were very religious and like so many devout Jewish women Mary would have been steeped in the traditional Jewish belief of the coming of a Messiah whose arrival would free the people of Israel from the darkness of sin. On the surface of things Mary seemed no different from any other girl of her age in the village. Little did anyone realise that she had a special place in the heart of God who preserved her from original sin from the very first moment of her conception in the womb of Saint Anne. Mary only became aware of her special position when as a teenager the angel Gabriel came into her life and placed before her the choice of accepting God's will and becoming the mother of his Son.

The fact that Mary was chosen by God to bring Jesus into the world meant that she had to be sinless from the very first moment of her life. It was only fitting that God should adorn Mary, from the first instant of her existence, with every kind of grace. The gospel shows how blissfully unaware Mary was of her privileged position and deep-rooted closeness to God. When the angel Gabriel spoke the words, 'Rejoice so highly favoured! The Lord is with you', she was puzzled as to what was the meaning of the greeting. This blessed girl who brought Jesus into the world had absolutely no pretensions. The good news that she was to become the mother of Christ proved too much for Mary. No doubt her thoughts would have been on ordinary domestic things like her impending marriage to Joseph to whom she was engaged and on how that would involve the leaving of her parents' house to set up a home of her own. She was deeply disturbed by the news, and did not feel the least bit adequate for the task she was being given. Moreover she had to discern whether or not this was God's will. On expressing her concerns to the angel, she was told not to worry, that everything was in the hands of God who would work wonders in her life.

When Mary said 'Yes' to the angel, she placed her life completely in the service of God and set in motion God's eternal plan to bring salvation to the human race. The annunciation was such a momentous occasion in salvation history that spiritual writers talk of heaven holding its breath as the redemption of the world hung upon the 'Yes' of a young maiden from Nazareth. Giving her consent did not mean the end of her worries. Mary would continue to be deeply disturbed and know sorrow as she pondered in her heart the many mysterious happenings that would come her way in the course of being a mother to Christ. Ahead of her lay exile in Egypt, her son's death on Calvary and her presence in the new community of believers as it explored the meaning of Christ's life, death and resurrection. In human terms there would be many occasions when all that she hoped for and dreamt about after the angel Gabriel's visit would collapse in smithereens before her very eyes. The sword of sorrow foretold by Simeon would pierce her through and through. Nevertheless, in spite of her inner conflict caused by everything shrouded in mystery she would continue to trust. What gave value to all she said and did was her unswerving obedience to God. She never went back on her word. Mary was above all a woman of faith. As a woman who experienced suffering in all its forms, Mary is God's gift to a broken world. On this her feastday we rejoice that there existed a member of our race whose total openness to God provided him with the opportunity of walking among us and offering us salvation.

Prayer of the Faithful

Celebrant: We now pray to God our Father that all who follow him in faith will readily listen to his voice and respond with an open heart.

1. That the church leaders and religious who are called to challenge God's people may never shirk their responsibility to preach the truth.
   Lord, hear us.

2. May all Christians find in the example of Mary the courage to say 'Yes' to God when asked to make a sacrifice for the sake of others.
   Lord, hear us.

3. For all children that the maternal love of the Mother of God may shield them from harm and keep them safe.
   Lord, hear us.

4. That the sick in their pain of mind and body may be strengthened by the goodness of those who care for them.
   Lord, hear us.

5. For our families and friends who have died, that God will keep them in the eternal peace and company of Mary our mother.
   Lord, hear us.

Heavenly Father, in your immense love for us you have given us Mary as our Mother and model to be with us at every turn on the river of life. Through her intercession, make us open to change. We ask this through Christ, our Lord. Amen.

Mission Sunday
First Reading: Deuteronomy 30:15-20;
Second Reading: 1 John 5:5-13; Gospel: John 6:48-51

We read in the Acts of the Apostles 4:1-21 how Peter and John were arrested in Jerusalem and imprisoned overnight by the Sadducees for preaching the resurrection of Jesus. The following day when brought before the Sanhedrin to explain their conduct they were cautioned about their behaviour and promised their freedom provided under no circumstances would they ever mention the name of Jesus again. Their reply, 'We cannot but speak about what we have seen and heard,' is proof that from the very beginning the desire to proclaim Jesus Christ as Lord was an essential part of what it means to be a Christian. The great commission to 'Go and make disciples of all nations, baptising them in the name of the Father, Son and Holy Spirit' given by Christ at the Mount of Olivet shortly before his ascension into heaven, is the church's reason for existing. The response of the apostles to that commission was an immediate and a consuming passion for the salvation of the world. They gave up the comforts of family life in order to commit themselves totally to the good news and become fearless messengers of the Lord. The Holy Spirit had filled them with a compelling desire to announce that we are all part of the worldwide, age old, family of God. On Mission Sunday we thank God for the faith of those early Christians who took the gospel command seriously and put it into practice. Had they not reached out, accepted the challenge and proclaimed what Jesus taught them, the church would never have come into being. Without the witness and enthusiasm of those close friends of Jesus, the good news would be absent from today's world. Despite the difficulties besetting them, these disciples set out and journeyed thousands of miles over land and sea spreading the message of eternal salvation, which had wrought such a change in their own personal lives.

Missionary activity as we know it has changed greatly over the years. Gone are the days when the missionary worked in the wake of a conquering army, when faith and sword went hand in hand with the imposition of an alien culture. Thankfully we have come to realise that God's spirit is present and alive in every unfolding situation. Mission is about making the world a better place for peoples of all creeds and none. It begins by recognising our common brotherhood and that we cannot live in a cosy little world looking after our own needs while the majority of our brothers and sisters cry out to God for the bare necessities of life. The missionary is now a stranger in another man's culture and appreciates the importance of adapting to the ways, customs and language of the people he serves. Today's missionaries are more likely to be among the preservers of local and tribal cultures, often collecting their myths, ritual customs and songs because they are aware of their innate sacredness. Their way of life is demanding, often fraught with danger but at the same time very fulfilling on a personal level. As one retired missionary reminiscing on a life's work in Nigeria recently wrote, 'We swam the rivers, climbed the mountains, learned the languages and taught the people the good news – that God is a God of love who dwelt among us and died for our sins. That was very good news for them. It lifted a stone from their hearts, banishing the endemic fear of evil spirits and witchcraft. Meanwhile we built schools and clinics, sank innumerable wells, and taught better agricultural methods. Or again helped to provide the basic needs of food and shelter often in the shadows of natural disaster or war.'

Mission Sunday reminds us of the roots of our faith and of the responsibility we carry to keep that faith alive and to offer it to others. The mission of Jesus means reaching out to embrace everyone, even those who do not believe. It is being God's presence for those struggling to be loved, his healing for those who are spiritually sick and his hope for those cut off and in the darkness of despair. All over the world the work of the gospel continues relentlessly. If knowing Jesus is worthwhile for us, we should commit ourselves personally to making him known. We could offer our prayers and our sufferings for some missionary we know. The important thing is to realise that we are called to play an active part in the church's task of winning souls for Christ. Everyone can and should be a missionary.

Prayer of the Faithful

Celebrant: We pray to God our Father that all the ends of the earth may find salvation in the name of his Son, Jesus Christ.

1. We pray that the church missionary may become a beacon of light in spreading the love of God throughout the world.
   Lord, hear us.

2. We pray for all missionaries, especially those who have borne the burdens of the day and grown old in the service of the Lord.
   Lord, hear us.

3. For the young churches in Asia and Africa. May the Spirit of God stir up a new energy in them for the good of the whole people of God.
   Lord, hear us.

4. That all who are frail or elderly may have the companionship of friends, the love of family, and the means to meet their needs.
   Lord, hear us.

5. That the dead, especially those we have known, may find peace with God in the heavenly community.
   Lord, hear us.

Heavenly Father, the zeal of missionaries has won many people for the church. May the good news proclaimed in his name help us to grow in love. We make our prayer through Christ, our Lord. Amen.

Emigrant Sunday

About seven years ago I was invited by my bishop to go to France as an emigrant chaplain to serve the Irish community in Paris – a community which numbers some twenty thousand people. I was taking over from another priest who had been stationed there for the previous six years. I was told that it would not be an easy posting as I would be very much on my own and he added that wherever there is a sizeable group of Irish people there should be an Irish priest with them. I mention that by way of introduction as today is Emigrant Sunday and we are asked to pray for family members, neighbours and friends who have had to seek their livelihood abroad and away from home.

Emigration has been a way of life for Irish people since famine times when exiles left with nothing more than the clothes on their back and barely enough money in their pocket to see them through the following week. Until they got properly settled and were able to carve out a life for themselves, they depended on Irish people who had emigrated before them to fix them up with digs and a job. This common bond of Irishness got the new arrivals on their feet and once they were up and running the majority were highly successful and made an enormous contribution to the land of their adoption. The pain of unimaginable hardship has now gone out of emigration because London, Paris and New York are but a few hours away and our young people are, by and large, better educated, less dependent on the pick and shovel and more aware of the realities of life. They are able to compete with the best and get decent jobs. Working in another country brings them new experience, and adds to their skill. They can return home more often, visit family and friends at Christmas, and talk about returning for good if the right opportunity arises.

And yet the picture is not all rosy or sunshine. Many young people experience loneliness and homesickness and feel insecure and isolated because of the loss of the familiar, of friends, family and loved ones. Being uprooted causes great pain. You gradually realise that at home you are somebody with your place in the community but away from home you are a nobody. Many of the songs and ballads of Ireland have emigration as their theme and become real tear-jerkers at Irish gatherings abroad. We are told that the pain of exile in London and the wanting to be back home inspired W. B. Yeats to write the poem called the *Lake Isle of Inishfree*. On Christmas day for the last six years I joined a group of emigrants for dinner in a hostel and despite the brave face being put on things all of them were hurting. Family was the big thing that was lacking. You could see from the flow of the conversation and the way they were describing Christmas at home and around their family table that they were all missing the warmth, cosiness and security of parents, brothers and sisters.

And then there are the misfits – people who can't cope on their own and who should never have left home. And I am thinking of Paul from Belfast whom I visited in jail every week. And red haired Michael from Navan, who knelt and begged on the boulevard St Michel with a slogan around his neck, 'Have pity on me, I am Irish.' And then there was John from Tipperary town who died of hypothermia in a bus shelter on Christmas Day three years ago. His family told me that he always phoned home and kept in touch but they never knew that he was living rough on the streets. All were very intelligent and had left home for various reasons but they never quite made it and remained on the periphery of society. And recent research shows that the Irish in Britain form a larger proportion of the homeless population than any other ethnic group. They also have a higher rate of mental illness and account for a disproportionately large number of suicides.

However emigration is not something peculiar to the Irish people. It is a world problem and as old as humankind. Even the Holy Family were exiles and refugees in Egypt during the time of King Herod. Patrick, our patron saint, was forcefully brought to our shores as a slave boy. But we do have obligations in charity and compassion to keep in touch with our own people. What matters is that they have our support, that we keep in touch with them, make that call or write that letter that we promised we would write and haven't yet got around to doing. When she was President of Ireland, Mary Robinson kept a light burning brightly in the window of her home in memory of emigrants. President Mary McAleese has retained that tradition of the lighted candle.

Today in church as a community we are asked to pray for emigrants that the Lord will guide them and protect them, and when we go home we are invited to keep their memory burning brightly in our hearts, in our minds and in our families.

Prayer of the Faithful

Celebrant: We make our prayer to God the Father, whose own Son knew the pain of exile as an infant refugee in Egypt.

1. We pray for all who have been forced to earn their daily bread abroad. May we ease their pain of separation and loneliness by keeping in touch with them.
   Lord, hear us.

2. That our civic leaders and those who hold public office may have the courage to address the injustices in our midst.
   Lord, hear us.

3. We pray that those who work with emigrants may have encouragement and support in their work.
   Lord, hear us.

4. May emigrants, who have lost their way and are living aimlessly, draw strength from the knowledge that Jesus has a special place in his heart for outsiders.
   Lord, hear us.

5. We pray for the dead and we remember especially those members of our own community who have died in their new homeland. When life's journey is over may we be reunited with them in our heavenly home.
   Lord, hear us.

Lord God, our guide and protector, support us in our work, be our strength in times of sorrow and come to our help in those wrenching moments of parting and saying goodbye. We make our prayer through Christ, our Lord. Amen.

Thematic Index